A fresh look at the C

LOVING

GOD'S

WAY

Gary DeLashmutt

New Paradigm Publishing, Columbus, Ohio 43229

Published 1996, 2015, 2024

Printed in the United States of America

Unless otherwise indicated, Scripture quotations are form the New American Standard Bible © the Lockman Foundation 1960, 1962, 1963, 1968, 1971, 1972, 1973, 1975, 1977.

ISBN 978-1-963358-07-0 (Paperback)

ISBN 979-8-9885087-8-6 (E-Book)

Cover design by Taylor Hicks

Typesetting by Silas Young

NEW PARADIGM

To my wife, Bev, who consistently
models so many of the truths
described in this book.

Contents

Preface

When a culture rejects the true God, one of the most tragic results is the destruction of community. Without the anchoring security of God's love and the knowledge of God's truth, people tend to become more and more self-centered. Their relationships with one another therefore become increasingly unhealthy and destructive. Today, western culture is experiencing this devastating consequence of rejecting the God of the Bible.

As those who have put our trust in Christ, we are called to express the love and truth of God to our culture. To do this we need to express something of the quality of community God has intended for human beings. Because our relationships with God have been restored, we can now learn how to relate to each other with love and truth as God intended. Through Christian community, we can show our culture that in Jesus Christ there is a way out of its relational lostness.

But we will not have perfect community, just as we will not have perfection in any area of our lives, until Christ returns. Although we are to be a real expression of God's family, Christian community still bears the marks of a fallen race. Our relationships with one another will be marred by sin—sometimes to an excruciating extent.

We need to put aside all utopian expectations if we hope to profit from our involvement in Christian community. We will not find parents who will give us the love we never received as children. Instead, we will find that God's love is sometimes expressed through his imperfect people in ways that help us to understand him better and trust him more as our heavenly Father.

We will never find relationships without reciprocal sin and pain and disappointment. Instead, in such relationships we will find opportunities to learn from God how to repent and forbear and forgive and persevere. We will not find leaders who always have answers and never make mistakes. Instead, we will find sinful people who model what it means to admit their mistakes and keep following Christ.

This book doesn't focus on how other people should treat us or how badly others are failing us. If you are like me, this perspective comes naturally when you think about relationships. We most naturally ask questions like, "How are you loving me? Are you meeting my needs the way you should be?" This focus destroys relationships.

God has a radical answer for such questions. He says, "I love you. I'm in your life now. I'm committed to love you fully and to the end. You don't have to look to other people and demand they meet your needs, because I'm going to take care of you. It's going to be an exciting adventure to trust me and then see how I meet your needs, sometimes directly and sometimes through the agency of my people."

Based on God's commitment to love us in this way, we should ask very different questions. "Am I willing to receive all forms of biblical love, not just the kinds that I like to receive? Am I willing to learn how to give all forms of biblical love to Christians, not just the kinds I enjoy giving?" If you answer these questions affirmatively, God will work through Christian community to change your life for good, and to make you a more effective influence for Jesus Christ.

This book is not about finding the right church structure. Many different structures facilitate Christian community, and each local church must choose those structures that will help true community develop. The heart of Christian community, however, is not structure. It is the commitment of its members to love one another as Christ loves us. My hope is that this book will help you to better understand what this kind of love looks like, and that it will motivate you to become a better contributor in your current Christian relationships.

1

The Importance of Christian Fellowship

*A new command I give you: Love one another. As I have loved
you, so you must love one another.*
John 13:34

In this book, we will be studying the "one another" passages of the New Testament letters. There are many ways of studying Christian love, but this approach is biblical, practical, and balanced. These passages are the best way to understand what Jesus meant in his own "one another" command: "Love one another. As I have loved you . . ." (John 13:34).

Jesus' disciples knew how to apply this command because they had lived with him for more than three years, experiencing and observing his love firsthand. But other first-century Christians, like us, did not have the benefit of this unique experience. To fill this gap, the apostles described distinctively Christian love in these "one another" passages. By studying these passages, then, we will build an understanding of love that is rooted squarely in the Bible, rather than in our culture's inadequate and changing views of love. We will learn what it means to love God's way.

This way of studying Christian love is also practical. There is nothing abstract or theoretical about commands like "forgive one another," "encourage one another," and "admonish one another." We cannot reflect on these passages without being challenged to change the way we relate to other people. Only the most self-centered reader could pervert them into a standard of how others must treat him, because they are addressed to each of us. The Bible does not say: "Be sure others forgive you," but rather: "You should forgive one another." You will likely discover that your relationships with other Christians are not what they should be, but you will also discover concrete ways to improve.

Finally, this approach to Christian love is balanced. Christ's love is multifaceted because it is rooted in the multifaceted character of God, and because human beings and life are complex. Jesus always related to others in love, but he expressed that love in very different ways as the need of the situation required. He wants us to cultivate this ability. For example, the command to encourage one another is important, but it does not cover all situations in life. Many situations call for admonition rather than encouragement. Furthermore, each of us will find ourselves drawn to some expressions of Christian love and repelled by others. Those which repel us often expose soft spots in our character development that need special attention. Studying the "one another" passages will help us to spot these areas and improve them with God's help.

Personal Perspective

God insists that we apply biblical truth if we want to experience its life-changing power. Learning to love one another obviously involves a commitment to relationships with other Christians. This is where the theological rubber meets the road—and what a hard road it can be! My own initial experience with Christian fellowship was a great struggle for me, but it has yielded even greater benefits.

I became a Christian a few weeks before I graduated from high school. Alone in my bedroom one night and in a rare moment of honesty, I realized that my life was going nowhere fast. Even though I had lots of friends and stimulation, I knew I was lonely and directionless. As I admitted this to myself, a passage from the Bible came to mind, a passage that a Christian friend had shared with me some months previously. I didn't know where it was in the Bible, but that didn't matter. It was the promise Christ made that arrested me: "Here I am! I stand at the door and knock. If anyone hears my voice and opens the door, I will come in and eat with him, and he with me" (Rev. 3:20). I decided to open the door of my heart, telling Christ that I would follow his direction for my life if only he would lead me.

Fast-forward nine months. I was alone in my bedroom again. This time I was crying out to Christ, telling him I had never been more lonely and miserable than I had been in the last nine months. This time, instead of asking Christ to come into my life, I asked him to leave. But Christ did not leave. Instead, he confronted me. He didn't speak with an audible voice, but I am certain he spoke to me at that moment. His message was a painful rebuke: "Why are you tying my hands? Why are you refusing to let me help you through my people?"

My involvement with other Christians since I had received Christ had been superficial and sporadic. I occasionally attended Bible studies that were large enough to allow me to avoid meaningful conversation with others. I usually arrived late and left early. Like most new Christians, I was biblically illiterate, so the teachings raised more questions than they supplied answers. While I asked God to explain his Word, I never asked another Christian to answer my questions. During those nine months, I never told another Christian any of my spiritual or personal struggles. In fact, I never interacted with other Christians on any meaningful level.

I was on a self-imposed slow-learning track, and my own pride was the primary reason for my lack of spiritual progress. As I looked around during those Christian gatherings, I inevitably saw many people who were "uncool" in my eyes. There was always something wrong with them: they were the wrong age, they dressed the wrong way, or their personalities turned me off. I was also too proud to ask questions about the Bible because doing so would betray my ignorance. I was trying to walk with Christ by myself and, as a result, the spiritual life that had germinated when I received Christ was diminishing as the doubts and dissatisfaction grew.

Christ brought me to a point of decision that night. He didn't make the decision for me, but he clarified the decision I needed to make. He called on me to quit tying his hands and he confronted me with my need to interact with other Christians in a vulnerable and meaningful way. In the years since that night, it has become clear to me that this decision to become involved with Christ's people has been one of the most significant in my life.

For me, the first steps were to ask the questions I had and to share some of my personal doubts and fears. This, of course, was frightening, but it made a striking difference in my relationship with Christ. I discovered I was not the only one who struggled—and that answers were available. My loneliness slowly subsided and the confidence that God was at work in my life gradually increased.

When I moved into a Christian ministry house, my spiritual life flourished even more. I felt closer and more connected to my housemates, and I profited immensely from the informal spiritual discussions and prayer. Shortly thereafter, I responded. Paul explains why this is so in Romans 12. In verse 3, he writes, "For by the grace given me I say to every one of you: Do not think of yourself more highly than you ought, but rather think of yourself with sober judgment, in accordance with the measure of faith God has given you." The word translated "sober judgment" literally means "psychologically sane."[1] Psychological health involves having an accurate view of ourselves. The importance of having a correct self-concept is not a modern discovery; it is something God has emphasized all along.

How do we form a proper self-concept? Primarily by understanding who we are according to God's design and then acting consistently with that design. As we read through the New Testament, we find God constantly informs us of who we are because of our relationship with Christ, and then urges us to take certain steps that are consistent with who we are. As we act consistently with what God says about us, our experiential confidence in God grows. For example, he tells us we are now permanently acceptable in his sight.

On that basis, he calls on us to draw near to him in personal fellowship regardless of how unworthy we may feel (Hebrews 10:19-22). As we choose to do this (often against our feelings), our experiential confidence in God's unconditional acceptance increases. If, however, we wait until we feel acceptable before we draw near to God, our confidence in God's acceptance will remain subject to our fluctuating behavior and moods.

In Romans 12, Paul tells us another key to a proper self-concept is understanding how we are related to other Christians. He explains this by way of analogy in verses 4 and 5: "Just as each of us has one body with many members, and these members do not all have the same function, so in Christ we who are many form one body, and each member belongs to all the others."

The organs of our physical bodies are clearly in an interdependent relationship with each other. Although each organ is a unique individual, its identity is also corporate. In fact, it discovers and expresses its individuality in its relationships with the other organs. Each organ needs the contribution of the other organs, and each organ needs to make its contribution to the other organs. In a healthy and growing body, each organ acts consistently with its identity. Should any organ begin to function contrary to this identity, physical sickness is sure to follow.

Imagine for a moment that your physical organs have the capacity of self-awareness, free choice, and self-expression. Suppose your liver, for example, didn't agree with the corporate aspect of its identity. What if it decided, "I feel confined by these other organs–they are impairing my growth as an individual! I want to be free to be me?" Or what if it decided, "I feel like I'm an unnecessary appendage. It doesn't matter whether I contribute anything to this body–it'll be fine without me?"

If your liver began to believe either of these assertions and acted consistently with these beliefs, you would be dead in a short time. Regardless of what your liver believes, it is a member of your body. As such, it needs the contribution of your other physical organs, and it makes a vital contribution to the overall health of your body.

What would you say to your liver? You would probably say something similar to what Paul says in this passage: "Don't be a megalomaniac. You are neither self-sufficient nor superfluous. You are an interdependent member of this body, and you need to act consistently with this fact."

What's the point of this review of human anatomy? Just this: What we understand and affirm about our own physical bodies, we often deny about ourselves as Christians. For a variety of reasons, many of us do not agree with God that we are interdependent members of the spiritual body of Christ.

Regardless of what we believe or feel about this issue, however, God's Word says we are members of the body of Christ. This identity does not threaten our individuality. We each have a unique relationship with the Head, Jesus Christ, and we each have a unique role to play in his purpose. But each of us is only one member, not the whole body. And we will have no more spiritual health apart from interdependent relationships with other Christians than our livers will have physical health apart from their connection with our other organs. This is the way we are, whether we believe it or not. This is our identity.

Because this is our identity, we need to act consistently with it if we want to be spiritually healthy. Because we are interdependent members of Christ's body, we need to allow Christ to give us his life and love and truth to us through other Christians, and we also need to allow him to give the same things through us to other Christians. God is not going to change the way he works to accommodate our ignorance or stubbornness. Instead, he seeks to correct our understanding of who we are through his Word, and then he challenges us in personal ways to start acting consistently with who we are.

This is exactly what I experienced as a new Christian. I was telling God to enable me to grow spiritually as an isolated, autonomous Christian. He was calling on me to acknowledge my interdependent identity. The breakthrough came when I decided to view myself as a member of his body and take my place as a member willing to receive and give.

Effective Evangelistic Impact

We also need involvement in Christian fellowship for the sake of those who don't know Christ. All Christians know that God wants people to have the opportunity to know him through Jesus Christ. Most Christians also realize God gives them the privilege and responsibility of extending this invitation to non-Christians. Surprisingly few Christians understand that Christian fellowship is a key component of Jesus' evangelistic strategy. He emphasized this component in John 13-17.

On the night of his arrest, Jesus spent several hours alone with his disciples. During this time, he shared with them the truths most important for them to remember. He said he was going away, but the Holy Spirit would continue to mediate his presence and guidance to them (John 14:1-29; 16:5-24). He told them they needed to continue to depend on him if they wanted to live effectively for him (John 15:1-16). And he expressed his desire for all people to come to know God by believing in him and his sacrifice for their sins. In this context, he also explained the role of Christian fellowship.

In John 13:34-35 Jesus said, "A new command I give you: Love one another. As I have loved you, so you must love one another. By this all men will know that you are my disciples, if you love one another." Jesus closed his discussion with the disciples in John 17 by praying. He prayed first for himself, he prayed next for those who were in the room with him, and then in verses 20-23 he prayed for all succeeding generations of Christians until his return: "My prayer is not for them alone. I pray also for those who will believe in me through their message . . ." He made a request for us: ". . . that all of them may be one, Father, just as you are in me and I am in you. May they also be in us so that the world may believe that you sent me. . . . May they be brought to complete unity to let the world know that you sent me and have loved them even as you have loved me."

Do you see Jesus' point? The quality of Christian fellowship commends the message of Christianity in a unique way. Sharing the message of God's love and grace is crucial. Intellectual persuasion and historical evidence can be effective in sharing Christianity. A well-reasoned individual presentation of how we came to Christ also has its place. Demonstrating personal integrity in your dealings with non-Christians is also important. But when non-Christians see Christians love each other in the distinctive ways that Jesus loved his disciples, they will be much more likely to personally come to Christ.

Why is this? In some ways, the relationship between Christian fellowship and evangelism is like the relationship between the lyrics and the music in a good song. If the music is boring or discordant, I rarely pay any attention to the lyrics. But if the music is interesting and attractive, I usually listen carefully. Christian fellowship is the music that attracts people to listen to the lyrics of the gospel. Most people are acutely aware of their desire to have healthy personal love relationships. When they are attracted to the "music" of Christians living in restored relationships with each other, they also often become attracted to the "lyrics" that tell them they can be restored to a relationship with God through Christ. Christian author John White puts it this way:

> God's plan is that local bodies of believing Christians, functioning as loving and caring units, provide a dynamic community in which both personal witness and evangelistic communication become intensely productive. The church that convinces people that there is a God is a church that manifests what only a God can do, that is, to unite human beings in love. . . . There is nothing that convinces people that God exists or that awakens their craving for him like the discovery of Christian brothers and sisters who love one another. . . . The sight of loving unity among Christians arrests the non-Christian. It crashes through his intellect, stirs up his conscience and creates a tumult of longing in his heart because he was created to enjoy the very thing that you are demonstrating.[2]

The late Christian philosopher and author Francis Schaeffer had the same conviction that genuine fellowship is essential for effective evangelism. He said,

> As Christians we must not minimize the need to give honest answers to honest questions. We should have an intellectual apologetic [a defense of our faith]. . . . Yet, without true Christians loving one another, Christ

says the world cannot be expected to listen, even when we give proper answers. Let us be careful indeed . . . to give honest answers. For years the . . . church has done this very poorly. . . . But after we have done our best to communicate [these answers], still we must never forget that the final apologetic which Jesus gives is the observable love of true Christians for true Christians.[3]

Conclusion

God wants us to experience his love, his forgiveness, and his guidance, and he offers this largely through other members of the Body of Christ. He is not going to change this truth of the importance of Christian fellowship for you or for me. Choosing to be a self-sufficient and selfish Christian is choosing to live a spiritually anemic and impoverished life. God is not going to take away our free will. Rather, he will confront us and ask, "When are you going to quit tying my hands? When are you going to quit preventing me from helping you through my people? When are you going to quit preventing me from helping my people through you?" Your own relationship with Jesus Christ will be impoverished unless you affirm this identity in your behavior as well as in your mind. But that's not all. Your decision will also affect other people's lives. That is the way reality works according to God. This is why your decision about this issue is so important.

Discussion Questions

1. What reasons do you use to avoid meaningful involvement with Christians?

2. Do you agree that choosing to act consistently with biblical truth is essential for experiencing its power in your life? Share other examples of this principle.

3. How have you seen Christian community result in effective evangelism? What role did it play in your own conversion? What about others who have come to Christ?

2

How Involved Should I Be?

*. . . we, who are many, are one body in Christ, and individually
members one of another.*
Romans 12:5

Once we become convinced of the importance of Christian fellowship, it is
only natural to ask, "How involved should I be?" Unfortunately, Christians
often answer this question in terms of the number of meetings we should attend
each week. We should not minimize the importance of assembling with other
Christians. Indeed, Hebrews 10:25 warns us not to "give up meeting together, as
some are in the habit of doing" (NIV). However, this is not an adequate answer
to the question. Christian fellowship involves something far more than attending
meetings. It is possible to attend many meetings a week, and yet not be involved
in true Christian fellowship. There are other situations in which Christians are
not able to meet together in groups because of physical illness or persecution.
Yet in spite of such conditions they experience some of the richest expressions
of Christian fellowship. The answer to the question "How involved should I be?"
must flow from the scriptural truths about Christian fellowship that we studied
in the previous chapter.

Experiencing Body Life

We should be involved enough with other Christians that we are regularly experiencing the fact that we are interdependent members of one another. This test applies in two distinct ways.

First, each of us needs to be able to say, "I am regularly accepting Christ's life from other Christians." This represents the receiving side of Christian fellowship. Some Christians think their need for supportive fellowship with other Christians is a sign of spiritual weakness. "If I were spiritually mature, I'd realize Jesus is the only one I need." There is an element of truth in this statement. According to the Bible, Jesus is indeed the only one we need. He alone is able to meet all of our deepest needs for security, meaning, direction, and significance. That is why we should be careful not to expect other human beings to fully meet these needs. Such dependence is a form of idolatry that will disappoint us. We also need to spend time alone with Jesus to cultivate relational closeness with him.

The fact remains, however, that Jesus chooses to meet many of our needs through the agency of other Christians. Since this is the case, we need to regularly initiate involvement with other Christians in ways that allow this to happen. This is why Paul, using the metaphor of the body warns us, "The eye cannot say to the hand, 'I don't need you!' And the head cannot say to the feet, 'I don't need you!'" (1 Corinthians 12:21 NIV). Many Christians prefer to speak of this kind of involvement as body-life because this term expresses the kind of interdependence Paul insists should be normative for us as members of Christ's spiritual body. "Going to church" weekly is a very different level of involvement than body-life.

It is also interesting that Paul, arguably the most spiritually mature Christian who ever lived, viewed involvement with other Christians as an ongoing need in his own life. Whenever we meet Paul in the book of Acts or in his letters, he is always with other Christians.[1] In one situation, a ministry crisis necessitated a temporary separation from his Christian friends. Referring to this incident, Paul said, "*So when we could stand it no longer*, we thought it best to be left by ourselves in Athens" (1 Thessalonians 3:1 NIV, italics added). For Paul, being alone (without Christian friends) was the last resort!

Are you able to identify the people through whom Jesus has given you spiritual support in the last couple of weeks? Are you able to say this has become an important part of your life, and that you keenly sense when it is absent? Is the prospect of being isolated from Christian friends something that would take a crisis for you to willingly endure? If you can honestly answer yes to these questions, you are experiencing your identity as a member of Christ's body. You are involved in an important feature of body-life.

Second, we should also be able to say increasingly, "I am regularly giving Christ's life to other Christians." This is the contributing side of involvement in Christian fellowship. God wants us to give his life to others as well as to receive his life through them. To this end, he has gifted each Christian to play a unique role in building up other Christians. Some are gifted to teach, some are gifted to administer, some are gifted to show mercy, some are gifted to encourage. When we exercise our spiritual gifts, we build up other Christians spiritually, and we experience the satisfaction that results from functioning in an area of God-given competence. To know our contribution is having a significant spiritual impact on others is part of our birthright as God's children. How sad it is that many Christians never experience this satisfaction!

How can we discover our spiritual gifts? In many different ways God reveals our ministry roles to us, and this normally occurs as a process rather than all at once. We will discuss this in greater detail later, but one thing is clear: We will discover our gifts only when we are involved with other Christians. God gives us spiritual gifts to build up other Christians. As we try to build up others, he will also affirm our areas of strength through the consistent feedback of other Christians who benefited from our service. But we will never get this sort of feedback unless we relate actively and regularly to other Christians.

Are you able to identify the Christians God has positively affected through you in the past few weeks? Do you have a better idea than you did a year ago of how God has gifted you to serve? Are you able to say giving Christ's life to other Christians is becoming an integral part of your life? Is the prospect of being unable to do this is increasingly distasteful to you? If you are able to answer yes to questions like these, you are involved in body-life!

Loving One Another

Another way to answer the question "How involved with other Christians should I be?" is to reflect on the practical implications of Jesus' command that we "love one another as I have loved you." As I stated at the beginning of this study, the apostles used "one another" passages to explain what it means to "love one another as I have loved you." The phrase one another describes a reciprocal relationship. That is, we are to give love to one another and we are to be willing to receive love from one another. Some of us like to give, but we feel uncomfortable receiving love from others. Some of us like to receive, but have trouble consistently giving love to others. There are many reasons why we are this way, and such tendencies don't change overnight. Authentic involvement in Christian fellowship, however, means that we have committed ourselves to learn how to both give and receive love. For this reason, our closest relationships should be with other Christians who have committed themselves to the same goal of growing in love. Those who relate only rarely or superficially with other Christians are not sufficiently involved. They may go to meetings, but they are not "in fellowship."

The "one another" imperatives also show us that God wants us to express love in many different ways. Some of these ways come more easily to us than others. For example, I may find it easy to admonish others, but difficult to encourage others. Is it all right to specialize in admonition? Not if I want the kind of involvement in Christian fellowship that God has designed for me. Instead, he will begin to alert me to opportunities to encourage others, and I need to be willing to practice this way of giving love that feels awkward to me. As we practice loving others in all the ways that Christ loves us, God will demonstrate his ability to change us and enrich our lives and the lives of others in ways we never thought were possible. In this context of a lifestyle built around self-giving love, God will also reveal our spiritual gifts and our unique ministry roles.

Warning: Hazards Ahead!

As you study this material, try to avoid two potential pitfalls. First, don't be a perfectionist with yourself. None of us will ever perfectly love one another the way Jesus loves us. This is always the goal, which means there is always room for improvement—but in this life we will continue to fall short of this goal. In fact, the people who are most effective at loving others are usually most acutely aware of how far short they fall! This is why we should cultivate genuine Christian fellowship in the soil of God's grace. God's grace forgives us and enables us to get back up and keep pursuing the goal of loving others more effectively.

Second, don't be a perfectionist with others. It is easy to pervert the "one another" imperatives into a merciless standard by which we evaluate others' attempts to love us. When we do this, we will begin to harbor resentment toward Christians who didn't love us as much as we think they should have, or in the ways we think they should have. Nothing will destroy Christian fellowship more quickly than this mentality. Others will never love us perfectly in this life. If we insist on all or nothing in our relationships with other fallen people, we will get nothing every time. This is why some of the most important "one another" commands are to "forgive one another" and "show forbearance to one another." When we seek to love others under God's grace–and give others that same grace as they relate to us–we will see God make our imperfect efforts into something more healing and meaningful than we could ever make by ourselves.

Discussion Questions

1. Assess your present involvement in Christian fellowship. Which is the greatest challenge for you–receiving or giving? What practical steps can you take to address deficiencies in your involvement?

2. Which form of perfectionism is a greater challenge for you–perfectionism with yourself or with others? What practical steps can you take to apply God's grace in this area?

3

Serve One Another

But I am among you as one who serves.
Luke 22:27

In the last chapter, we saw that Jesus laid down a new modus operandi for his followers: "A new command I give you: Love one another. As I have loved you, so you must love one another" (John 13:34). The questions facing us are "What does this kind of love look like, and how can we imitate it?"

We get a clue from the setting of this verse. It is the evening of Jesus' arrest. He has gathered his disciples to celebrate the Passover feast and he has explained that he is about to fulfill it through his death. The place is a secret second-floor room somewhere in Jerusalem. Jesus felt deeply burdened by the ordeal he was about to undergo, and he wanted to be with his closest friends. His disciples, meanwhile, were busy debating their favorite topic: "a dispute arose among them as to which of them was considered to be greatest" (Luke 22:24 NIV). At the very time that Jesus most desired their support, they were too busy exalting themselves to notice.

This ego battle created an awkward situation. Jewish custom dictated that guests' feet be washed when they arrived. This custom refreshed the guests and communicated love and respect. However, because the task was so lowly and menial, it was reserved for the household slaves. Evidently, there was no such slave present in the upper room. Since peers did not normally wash one another's feet,[1] whichever disciple did this would be automatically retracting his claim to be the greatest.

How would you respond if you were in Jesus' place? I would probably have let out a moan of disgust, or maybe I would have slammed my fist on the table and reamed them out with a scathing rebuke. Jesus' approach was different. John tells us that Jesus "got up from the meal, took off his outer clothing, and wrapped a towel around his waist. After that, he poured water into a basin and began to wash his disciples' feet, drying them with the towel that was wrapped around him" (John 13:4,5). Assuming the dress of a household slave, Jesus washed the dirt from each of his self-aggrandizing disciples' feet. He washed the feet of Judas, who he knew would soon betray him. He washed the feet of Peter, who he knew would soon deny him. When he finished, his towel skirt was brown with the filth of Jerusalem streets.

Then, in the embarrassed silence undoubtedly created by his actions, Jesus spoke to his disciples.

> Do you understand what I have done for you? . . . You call me 'Teacher' and 'Lord,' and rightly so, for that is what I am. Now that I, your Lord and Teacher, have washed your feet, you also should wash one another's feet. I have set you an example that you should do as I have done for you. (John 13:13-15)

To make sure they didn't miss his point, he also said this:

> The kings of the Gentiles lord it over them; and those who exercise authority over them call themselves Benefactors. But you are not to be like that. Instead, the greatest among you should be like the youngest, and the one who rules like the one who serves. For who is greater, the one who is at the table or the one who serves? Is it not the one who is at the table? But I am among you as one who serves. (Luke 22:25-27)

Through his example and through his words, he rejected the basis from which his disciples were operating. While he affirmed their desire to be great, he redefined the measure of true greatness. True greatness has nothing inherently to do with our position or title. The truest index of greatness is not how many people serve you; it is how many and how sacrificially you serve. When Jesus said shortly thereafter, "Love one another as I have loved you," the disciples knew this love involved serving one another.

In this context, Jesus made another statement that shatters our normal perspective on life. "Now that you know these things, you will be blessed if you do them" (John 13:17). "Blessed" in this context does not refer to some ethereal religious bliss. The Greek word (*makarios*) means "happy" or "fulfilled." Here is a recipe for personal happiness that is as "backward" as Jesus' definition of greatness! The world teaches us that we will be happy when we succeed in getting other people to love us and serve us as we desire. Jesus, however, says we will be happy when we learn how to consistently practice serving love toward others.[1] Our happiness in life is not ultimately subject to how others view and treat us—something over which we have no real control. It is rather a result of receiving Christ's love and then serving others in love.

Next to the amazing message of God's grace, this is the most revolutionary truth in the Bible. God's grace makes his love and acceptance available to us as a free gift, completely apart from all merit on our part. Through the loving service of his Son's death on the cross, God offers to "wash our feet" by cleansing us permanently from our sins. Then he promises us a life of fulfillment as we cultivate a lifestyle of giving our lives away to others for Jesus' sake. Truly, if we know these things, we will be fulfilled if we do them!

What does it mean to live a servant lifestyle? That is a big question. The Bible answers it in many ways. Servanthood involves the use of our gifts to build up the Body of Christ. It is also something we are to practice in the different arenas of our lives (marriage, family, work, church, etc.). More than anything else, though, servanthood is an attitude—a mindset. "Have this mindset in yourselves," said Paul, "which was also in Christ Jesus. . ." (Philippians 2:5). Many New Testament passages explain this attitude and contrast it with attitudes that oppose it.

Servanthood Versus Selfishness

Selfishness is obviously the opposite of a servant attitude. Paul says, "Do nothing out of selfish ambition. . ." (Philippians 2:3). To be selfish means to live for self—to make our wants the bottom-line consideration for our decisions. The selfish Christian is one who resists or avoids servanthood as a way of life. This way of life can express itself in a variety of ways.

Self-Protective Versus Other-Centered

Not long ago, I visited the city of Manaus in Amazonian Brazil. Walking downtown one night, I saw packs of young children—no older than twelve or thirteen—roving the streets. They were begging for money, trying to pick pockets, shoplifting, and beating up on each other. When I offered to buy a sandwich for one of them, he berated me and demanded money. I was appalled by this situation, and asked my Amazonian friend why these children were unsupervised. His answer shocked me. He said, "Oh, those are the 'throw-away' kids. Their parents didn't want them, so they abandoned them here in the city. Most of them have been on the street since they were five or six years old." In a moment, my perspective on these children shifted radically. While their behavior was no less objectionable, I understood better why they acted the way they did: They had no parents to take care of them. Abandoned in a hostile city, they had to take care of themselves to survive.

In a way, the "throw-away" kids of Manaus are a picture of humanity alienated from God. Born into a deeply fallen world, we are alone and struggling to survive in a hostile environment. This setting leads naturally to a self-protective, self-centered way of life. By the time I reached high-school age, I realized that most people (including myself) did not operate from altruistic motives. Those who didn't realize this got chewed up and spit out. I determined that I would survive by looking out for number one. Other people were predators to avoid or prey to use. I wasn't entirely comfortable with this philosophy of life, and I often couldn't live consistently with it, but I believed it was realistic.

The selfish Christian still operates from this same assumption: "I have to take care of me first. If I don't, who will?" The problem with this perspective, of course, is that as Christians we are no longer abandoned. God has adopted us into his family, and he now promises to care for us as his beloved children. This fact should fundamentally change the way we look at God, and the way we relate to others.

Imagine what it would be like if you adopted one of the "throw-away" children and brought him home. It would probably take some time for him to realize that he no longer had to relate to other people as he once did. You would probably catch him stealing money from your wallet. He would probably embarrass you by shoplifting when you took him to a store. His assumptions about life would be so deeply ingrained that they wouldn't change overnight. You would have explained to him repeatedly that it is no longer necessary to live as a predator-survivor, because you love him and will meet his basic needs. Hopefully, he would begin to believe you. What would be the proof that he did? As he saw the record of your faithfulness, he would begin to relax in the confidence that you were there for him. He would quit stealing food and money, because he'd realize it wasn't necessary any more. The real evidence that he was living as your adopted son would be that he'd begin to take an interest in how he could give to other people. Believing that his loving parents would meet his needs, he would begin to develop an interest in helping others.

How could Jesus be so other-centered with his disciples on the very night that he knew he would be arrested? Many Christians assume that since he was God, he simply "switched on his divine love." Jesus was indeed fully God, but the New Testament tells us that he lived as a human with the same limitations that we experience. He lived a life of perfect dependence on his Father. John tells us this was why he could be so other-centered on that night. "Jesus knew that the Father had put all things under his power, and that he had come from God and was returning to God; so he got up from the meal, took off his outer clothing, and wrapped a towel around his waist. After that, he poured water into a basin and began to wash his disciples' feet. . ." (John 13:3-5). Jesus knew that his life was secure in his Father's hands. Because he knew and believed this, he focused on how he could serve his disciples. This is the example he has left for us to follow.

Christians who live self-centered, self-protective lives are living in fundamental denial that they have a powerful and loving heavenly Father. When Jesus reproves us for being consumed with material anxiety, he bases his reproof on the fact that we have a Father who loves us and who has pledged to take care of us.

> Do not worry about your life, what you will eat or drink; or about your body, what you will wear. . ... Look at the birds of the air; they do not sow or reap or store away in barns, and yet your heavenly Father feeds them. Are you not much more valuable than they?. . . And why do you worry about clothes? See how the lilies of the field grow. They do not labor or spin. Yet I tell you that not even Solomon in all his splendor was dressed like one of these. If that is how God clothes the grass of the field, which is here today and tomorrow is thrown into the fire, will he not much more clothe you, O you of little faith? So do not worry, saying, 'What shall we eat?' or 'What shall we drink?' or 'What shall we wear?' For the pagans run after all these things, and your heavenly Father knows that you need them. (Matthew 6:25-32)

Jesus doesn't stop there. Our trust in God's care should not only gradually free us from worry; it should also free us to serve others. Luke records Jesus' conclusion when he spoke on the same subject: "Do not be afraid, little flock, for your Father has been pleased to give you the kingdom. [Therefore] sell your possessions and give to the poor. . ." (Luke 12:32,33). As an act of faith that God will take care of me, I should begin to think about how God may want to work through me to help others. "Each of you should look not only to your own interests, but also to the interests of others" (Philippians 2:3).

It is difficult to cultivate an other-centered thought-life. We naturally think about what we need and what we must do to get what we need. God, however, wants to teach us to trust him enough to think about the needs of others. His Spirit is able to remind us of God's faithfulness that he promises in his Word and demonstrates to us in our lives. He also regularly provides us with opportunities to help others, often when we feel consumed by our own needs. Our part is not only to respond to the opportunities God puts before us, but also to creatively "*consider* how we may stimulate one another on toward love and good deeds" (Hebrews 10:24). We need to make the choice to set our minds on the people God has brought into our lives, and prayerfully meditate on how we might influence them for good. As we cooperate with him in this process, we can gradually become people who are more and more genuinely other-centered—and more genuinely happy as well!

Owner Versus Steward

When we have a selfish perspective, we view ourselves as the owners of our lives. As owners, we choose our own agendas. The specifics of our agendas may vary widely, but the outcome is the same: This is *my* life, these are *my* things, and I use them to advance *my* purposes. When confronted with the needs of others, we feel comfortable saying "This doesn't fit into my agenda, so I refuse to consider it."

People have operated this way ever since Adam and Eve turned away from God—but until very recently society has viewed this attitude as immoral. People tended to relate to one another from selfish motives, but they would usually feel the need to defend their actions as based on some other, unselfish standard. It was rude and uncivilized to be overtly and unapologetically selfish. Within the last few decades, all that has changed in the western world. Today, our culture promotes egocentric living as a virtue! Experts offer seminars on self-assertiveness training, teaching us how to get what we want and ignore even the legitimate needs of others. They label those who adopt a serving lifestyle "dysfunctional" or "codependent." This is the age of "Self" magazine and talk-show hosts who act as high priests of the cult of Self. For the first time in human history, sociological and psychological well-being is being defined in blatantly selfish categories. As the Bible predicted, people are truly becoming "lovers of self" (2 Timothy 3:2), and the love of most people is growing cold (Matthew 24:12). This development is unleashing a level of alienation, brutality and misery never before witnessed in human history.

Of course, certain kinds of service can be unhealthy. We will explore some of these aberrations later in this chapter—but to throw the "baby" of servanthood out with the "bath water" of neurotic pseudo-service is both irrational and unbiblical. As Christ's followers, we should be deeply critical of this emphasis, ready to expose its emptiness by lives that display serving love. Tragically, many western Christians are instead naively gulping down this lie—and advocating it as well. Christian books that capitalize on how to build self-esteem, how to stop loving others too much, how to embrace your pain and admit your victimization, and how to set boundaries are hot copy. There is truth in many of these books, but often the main emphasis is profoundly unbiblical because they fail to advocate a lifestyle of serving love.

As Christians, we have entered into a personal relationship with the living God. By paying the penalty for our sins, Christ has purchased us for himself. "You are not your own; you were bought at a price. Therefore honor God with your body" (1 Corinthians 6:19,20). In view of the mercy God has lavished on us, we should acknowledge this fact and freely choose to give our lives to him. In other words, we should begin to consciously view ourselves as *stewards*. A steward is not an owner—he is a manager who is entrusted with his owner's possessions and charged with the responsibility to invest them for his purposes. This shift in how we view ourselves is foundational to a genuinely biblical lifestyle.

For Christian stewards, then, the ultimate consideration is not "What do I want?" but rather "What is God's will?" This is not some trite moralistic platitude—it is a conviction that Jesus practiced and calls us to practice as well. On the night of his arrest, Jesus agonized over the prospect of humiliation, physical torture and the unimaginable experience of bearing the fury of his Father's wrath for our sins. Although he had lived his whole human life aware that this was the purpose for which he came, he buckled under the weight of its imminence. All of his human instincts reacted against the demand that he sacrifice his life. He cried out in the faint hope that there was a way to avoid this fate—but he was answered only by his Father's silence and his own memory of scripture. Jesus displayed his greatness by reaffirming the conviction that directed his life: ". . . not what

I will, but what you will" (Mark 14:36). The steward mentality expressed in this prayer is the essence of all authentic prayer.

How do you respond when God contradicts your agenda with the needs of other people? Christian stewards continue to discover selfishness in their agendas, but they recognize this is inconsistent with loving God. Are you learning to say with Jesus, "I want God's agenda for my life, so I'm willing to subordinate my agenda to his." This doesn't mean we must say "Yes" to every request or demand that others make on us, but it does mean that we relinquish the right to decline simply because it doesn't fit into our self-chosen agendas. If we are embracing a steward identity, we will be able to see how God has regularly interrupted our agendas with his will to serve others. These interruptions are sometimes painful, and they will provide us with faint glimpses of Jesus' experience in Gethsemane. They will also lead the way to a life of increasing freedom and fulfillment.

Servanthood Versus Servility

Servility is a counterfeit form of servanthood. A servile person performs the outward actions of a true servant, but with the wrong attitude. If our fallen natures lose the battle to preserve a blatantly selfish lifestyle, they will likely resort to the tactic of promoting Christian servility. Servility has many faces that we need to be able to recognize if we want to cultivate authentically serving lives.

Bare-Minimum Versus Whatever It Takes

Most of us have developed beyond blatant selfishness to the point where we accept that fact that we have responsibilities to others. However, selfishness continues to underlie much of our "service" to others. For example, there is the "bare minimum" syndrome. Within the sphere of our accepted responsibilities, we do as little as possible to get by. Outside those responsibilities, we have no problem saying, "Don't inconvenience me!"

My grade-school daughters grudgingly accept their responsibility to clean their rooms, but they are often outraged if I ask them to help me clean any other room. "That's not my mess!" they protest, apparently oblivious to the fact that it's not my mess either. The idea of volunteering to do a job that falls outside their assigned duties seems like madness to them. I keep waiting for the day when they offer to do whatever it takes to keep the house in shape—but I'm not holding my breath. Parenting is slow work, in large part because children are so innately selfish.

What happens when we ask people at the work-place to help with a task that falls outside their job description? Most managers would love to have associates who consistently display a "can do" attitude. More often, though, associates greet them with an indignant pronouncement: "That's not my job!" Job descriptions are important, and we sometimes need to say "No" to others to fulfill our appointed duties. But the "bare-minimum" syndrome normally rules: Do your assigned work, don't volunteer, and decline requests for help.

Christian servants, if they are honest, regularly struggle with this mentality. God regularly convicts me of my laziness. Instead of "doing my work heartily as for the Lord rather than for man" (Colossians 3:23), I naturally tend to lope along at one-third speed unless other people get on me about it. For me, it is a constant challenge to go beyond my regular, scheduled responsibilities to look for additional ways I can serve. God provides me with these opportunities all the time, but I usually view them as obstacles to my assigned work or my cherished "free time." I do this, even though years of experience has taught me that serving beyond my "job description" is a key to enjoying my work and seeing God work through me in exciting ways.

As I was writing this chapter yesterday, I was "interrupted" by a request to visit a dying relative and talk with her about Christ. I am ashamed to admit how deeply aversive I was to this request. "I am behind on my work for this book (on Christian love!). This is not a ministry for which I am gifted. I am drained from working. I haven't gotten to relax during the holidays." As I reflected for a moment, a smile spread over my face. God certainly has a sense of humor! He was "calling my bluff" again and challenging me to subordinate my own wants to his desire to bless someone he loves. I was simultaneously sickened by my own selfishness, amazed by the grace of God, and (more slowly) excited about the prospect of showing God's love to a needy person. As I chose to exchange my "owner" posture for that of God's steward, I walked into a situation that was no less personally painful or awkward. I walked out once again thrilled by God's empowering and the joy that paradoxically results from sacrificial service.

With Strings Versus Freely

Most of us learn it is necessary to give to others to get along in life—but we usually give with strings attached. We often view serving others like investing our money in a lending institution: We want it back eventually, and with interest. The world is full of examples of this kind of pseudo-giving. Politicians regularly do favors for others, and then call those favors in as needed. Many married couples experience strife because they give with strings. When spouses keep a mental record of their service to one another, and are willing to recite that record when they don't get what they want, score-keeping replaces the basic dynamic of giving freely, and trouble is sure to follow. The temptation to give with strings is ever-present in Christian ministry as well. Jesus warns us against serving to be noticed by others because he knew how easily this motivation can corrupt our work for God (Matthew 6:1-18).

What is the evidence that we are giving with strings? Some people become angry when others deny their requests. "Fine! After all I've done for you lately! See if I help you again!" Consciously or sub-consciously, they feel that others are in debt to them for their service, so they are outraged at being ripped off. Others lose their motivation to continue serving because there isn't the payoff they expected. God will test our motives for Christian service at this point. No matter how sincere we may think we are, ministry will invariably surface "giving-to-get" motives. We don't get the recognition we feel we deserve. Other people have not responded to our input the way they should have responded. God has not enabled us to bear the fruit we had expected by this time. So we may conclude that it simply isn't worth it to serve others in the name of Christ.

How radically different God's way is!

> . . . if you lend to those from whom you expect repayment, what credit is that to you? Even 'sinners' lend to 'sinners,' expecting to be repaid in full. . . . But . . . do good to them, and lend to them without expecting to get anything back. Then your reward will be great. . . . Give, and it will be given to you. A good measure, pressed down, shaken together and running over, will be poured into your lap." (Luke 6:34-38)

Jesus calls on us to give without strings to others, trusting God to provide for us greater blessings than we could ever receive by mere repayment. In amazing ways and in his own timing, God promises to bless us as we give ourselves away to others for Jesus' sake. We may not dictate the terms or the timing; that is God for to decide. Our part is to trust his promise by giving freely.

Pride Versus Humility

Some Christians serve, but they do it with a "prima-donna" attitude. Highly gifted Christians are especially vulnerable to this mindset. Like athletes whose talents have gone to their heads, they have a way of communicating "I am a star on God's team, and you should feel privileged that I play for you." They act as if they have it all together, and don't need help from other Christians.

Most of us can't relate to this mentality. We're so acutely aware of our weaknesses and limitations that we'd like to have the prima-donna's problem for a while! We disqualify ourselves from opportunities to minister for Christ because we can't do what the highly gifted can do. In fact, most Christians decide they are so limited that it doesn't matter whether they serve others or not. Some even teach that this is a spiritual attitude.

Do you realize that this attitude is just as prideful as the prima-donna's? The prima-donna is prideful because he considers himself indispensable even though God's Word says he is only one member of Christ's Body. If, however, we act out the belief that we are insignificant members of Christ's body, isn't this also placing ourselves above what God says? The same Bible that rebukes a prima donna ("Do not think of yourself more highly than you ought. . . . Do not be proud, but be willing to associate with people of low position. Do not be conceited," Romans 12:3,16) also rebukes those who believe they have nothing to contribute ("If the foot should say, 'Because I am not a hand, I do not belong to the body,' it would not for that reason cease to be part of the body. And if the ear should say, 'Because I am not an eye, I do not belong to the body,' it would not for that reason cease to be part of the body" (1 Corinthians 12:15-16). Humility requires both that we allow God to help us through others, and that we assume our responsibility to make the contribution God wants us to make.

Have To Versus Get To

Sometimes we view service as something we have to do. We understand responsibility and doing the right thing, but we act like draftees rather than volunteers. We become duty-oriented. Our underlying mentality is "Even though this will be personally detrimental to me, I have to do it." When we have this mindset, we usually accompany our service with complaints of how difficult our lives are. This attitude may elicit pity, but it rarely inspires others to service!

The Bible sometimes talks about duty. Paul spoke of his commission as an apostle in this way in 1 Corinthians 9: "Yet when I preach the gospel, I cannot boast, for I am compelled to preach. Woe to me if I do not preach the gospel! If I preach voluntarily, I have a reward; if not voluntarily, I am simply discharging the trust committed to me." Sometimes, Paul served under orders. He knew what it meant to continue carrying the message of Christ to needy people even when he could think of other more appealing things to do. It will be the same with us if we decide to adopt a servant lifestyle. God has commissioned us to serve him in a certain capacity, and we are responsible to fulfill our role even when the going gets tough.

But Paul's attitude was not servile for one important reason: He was firmly convinced that God was always good to him. The servile Christian believes not just that service is sometimes painful; he believes it is not fundamentally good for him. It is slowly wearing him away, but he has to do it. It is his burden in life. Paul decisively rejected this perspective. He knew that God worked all things together for good for those who love him (Romans 8:28), that he would provide the resources needed to serve (Colossians 1:29), and that he would one day richly reward his servants (2 Timothy 4:8). Servile Christians, by contrast, mistrust God's goodness. They suspect he is ripping them off. They are like the prodigal son's older brother—serving faithfully, but secretly suspicious that his father doesn't care about him. This is why a sigh of resignation surrounds their service. They are serving an unloving master of their own imagination.

Knowing and affirming God's goodness transforms "have to" service into the real thing. When we remember that God has rescued us from condemnation, and when we meditate on the evidence of God's love for us, the Holy Spirit fills our hearts with a desire to thank God by serving others. This realization undergirded Paul's life and was the secret to his incredible perseverance. He viewed his apostolic commission as a privilege on par with the privilege of God's forgiveness. "I became a servant of this gospel by the gift of God's grace given me through the working of his power. Although I am less than the least of all God's people, this grace was given me: to preach to the Gentiles the unsearchable riches of Christ. . ." (Ephesians 3:7,8). The sacrifices of ministry were sometimes very heavy to Paul, but they never obscured his awareness of how privileged he was to serve a God who would love someone like him.

To Be Accepted by Others Versus Because Accepted by God

Many Christians serve others primarily to be loved and accepted by them. They need others' acceptance and approval because they don't operate from faith in God's acceptance. When this is our root motivation, Christian ministry is an extremely perilous enterprise. Some people reward our input with anger and rejection. Others ignore us even though we want them to like us. If we are in it to be accepted, we are in it to get more than to give—and this will skew our judgment on how to deal with people. We may hold back from reproving someone even though they need it, because we fear they will reject us. We may get angry when people don't appreciate all we've done for them. We may get jealous of other Christian workers because they receive the respect we so desperately crave. We may avoid the personal vulnerability that is necessary for effective discipleship because we worry that people will think less of us. We may become manipulative in extracting attention and affirmation from the younger Christians we should be encouraging. In a perverted, paradoxical way, we can begin to feed off the very people we should feed.

Recently, I was counseling a Christian worker who manifested these symptoms. When I asked him why he ministered, he replied, "To get my significance and identity." As he went on to say something else, I stopped and asked him if I heard him correctly. "Sure," he said, "Doesn't everybody?" I answered that God does indeed encourage us and affirm us through ministry, but this encouragement doesn't necessarily come from the people we're serving. It's more of an exhilaration that God has worked through us to bless another person, and a deep-down sense that he is faithful and good. However, if we depend on the people we serve to provide us with our significance and identity, we have become idolaters—seeking from others what only God can provide. Eventually, serving to be accepted polarizes us: Either we learn to take our acceptance from God in a deeper way, or we will manipulate weaker people to make us feel accepted, or we will forsake ministry.

It is excruciating to see this kind of selfishness in our hearts. Many react to this realization by withdrawing from Christian service until they perfect their motives. Since the alternative to service is selfishness, however, this medicine is worse than the disease. While we may need to step out of ministry roles that make it easy for us to give to get, God's way is for us to continue trying to help other people while we cooperate with his work to purify our hearts. Look for anonymous ways to serve. Serve those whose acceptance you do not crave. If you are willing to acknowledge the "giving to get" attitude when God exposes it, and then to take the steps in that direction that he'll surely reveal to you, you will gradually experience what it means to serve from the security of God's acceptance.

I don't know about you, but I wrestle with most of these attitudes on a regular basis. On the one hand, my fallen nature is constantly and creatively corrupting my service with selfishness and servility. On the other hand, the Holy Spirit is constantly exposing these counterfeits and calling on me to cooperate with him as an authentic servant. I live in the tension between these two influences—this is the normal Christian experience. "For the sinful nature desires what is contrary to the Spirit, and the Spirit what is contrary to the sinful nature. They are in conflict with each other, so that you do not do what you want" (Galatians 5:17). Sometimes I heed the Spirit's desire, and sometimes I don't. Spiritual maturity is not getting to the point where you no longer experience this tension. Rather, maturity is becoming more sensitive to it and choosing more consistently to trust the leadership and empowering of God's Spirit—by stepping out in the midst of fear, aversion, and inadequacy to serve.

Accepting Legitimate Limitations

Even when serving with substantially pure motives, Christians can get into trouble. Christian ministry is a life-long and extremely taxing lifestyle. God has designed us as finite and dependent beings. Unless we humbly acknowledge this fact and embrace God's support system for our lives, we easily become imbalanced servants who crash and burn instead of finishing the race.

Independent Versus Inter-dependent

Some Christian workers don't sufficiently acknowledge their need for others. They are usually other-centered in their outlook, consistent in fulfilling their responsibilities, and they rarely complain. Often, they are the most mature Christians in the group and are functioning as spiritual "parents" for many newer Christians. In this context, it is easy to become independent in an unbiblical sense. No matter how spiritually mature we are, we never outgrow our need for ongoing support and advice from colleagues. Prayer is necessary, but no amount of private prayer will make up for this kind of fellowship. Precisely because we are playing such crucial roles in the work, we need to maintain our spiritual health. It is admirable for a soldier to ignore a flesh wound when the battle rages. It is foolish, however, to slowly bleed to death because he refuses to "bother" the medics.

The best way to prevent this imbalance is to schedule regular time with colleagues for mutual edification. Grab all the spontaneous fellowship you can get, but unless you schedule regular times like this, you're probably malnourished. I find that I need several such times per week. Lean against your likely tendency to feel like you are burdening other workers, and ask for time. Then make use of this time by sharing your burdens, asking for advice, laughing together, encouraging one another, and praying for each other. These times become refueling stations strategically placed through the week.

Workaholics Versus Long Distance Pace

Some Christians demonstrate an admirable commitment to ministry, but they rarely take time to rest or exercise or recreate. They are Christian workaholics. It's not just that they are more temperamentally active than others; they feel guilty unless they are working. Unless they see a direct connection between what they are doing and Christian work, they feel they are wasting their time. They often critique those who engage in play—but they also tend to burn out, their bodies develop stress disorders, and their marriages break down.

Our culture rightly criticizes this way of life, but for the wrong reason. "Your problem is that you care about others too much. You don't love yourself enough." This is the wrong way to resolve the problem. God says the problem is never that we don't love ourselves enough. Although we are often mistaken about how to do so, we are always firmly committed to seek our own well-being. That's why he commands us to "love your neighbor as yourself."

Relaxation, exercise, rest and recreation are not rights to which we are entitled. They are responsibilities so that we can go the long haul in our service for God. While we should be willing to sacrifice these things when God calls on us to do so, we should still schedule them into our lives. They are part of God's provision that enables us to stay fit and healthy for him. We may need to cultivate the ability to enjoy relaxation and play as a part of our commitment to Christ! Changing life situations require that we periodically reevaluate and adjust our schedules to reflect this balance.

Messiah Versus One Member

Still others have real trouble saying "No" to needs that arise. They feel that unless they are the ones doing the serving, it just isn't getting done as well as it could. Because of their wealth of experience and maturity, they usually can do better than most people around them. Furthermore, there is often something very gratifying about knowing that others view them as indispensable.

Pastors who operate in churches that have clergy-laity expectations are usually especially vulnerable to this imbalance. Most members in this setting expect their pastors to do virtually all the "spiritual" work. This church functions like a football stadium in which 22 people are desperately in need of a rest, while 22,000 are desperately in need of activity!

The key biblical insight that speaks to this problem is Paul's statement in 1 Corinthians 12:14, "... the body is not made up of one part but of many." God has equipped each of us to play a key role in the church, but we cannot play everybody's role. I can do my part, but I must also call others to do their parts, and even allow work to go undone if others refuse to do it. Otherwise, I am playing messiah, and God will allow me to learn the hard way that I am not the whole body!

Conclusion

"You were called to freedom, brethren; only do not turn your freedom into an opportunity for the flesh, but through love serve one another" (Galatians 5:13). This is the choice that lies before us. Will we use our freedom in Christ to follow our culture's endless and futile quest for selfish gratification, or will we use it to cultivate a lifestyle of serving love? Next to receiving Christ, no other decision has more far-reaching consequences for ourselves and those we influence.

Discussion Questions

1. Which alternatives to servanthood do you wrestle with the most? What has been helpful in combating them?

2. What is the difference between biblical self-esteem and self-esteem according to our culture? What role does serving love play in these two views of self-esteem?

3. Share past examples when you experienced Christ's promise that serving love results in fulfillment. Share current examples in which you need to believe this promise.

4

Encourage One Another

. . .encourage one another and build one another up.. . .
1 Thessalonians 5:11

When learning to love one another, encouragement is a great place to start. Of all the "one another" imperatives which explain how to love one another, the New Testament letters use and advocate encouragement most often.[1] This gives us some idea of its importance in the minds of their authors. They were intent upon forming Christian communities rich in reciprocal encouragement.

The primary New Testament word for encouragement is *parakaleo*. *Parakaleo* means literally "to call alongside." Extra-biblical Greek authors sometimes used it to describe military situations in which soldiers were strengthened to fight on in battle.[2] True Christianity is a life of battle against spiritual forces of wickedness, against our fallen natures, and against a spiritually hostile and seductive world. In this environment, even mature Christians sometimes nearly lose hope, give way to their fears, or lapse into defeated lethargy. For such suffering Christians, biblical encouragement communicates God's truth and love in ways that strengthen them to go on following God's will for their lives. It is therefore a powerful spiritual influence in the Christian life.

God himself is the preeminent Encourager. Paul calls God the Father the "God of *all* encouragement" (2 Corinthians 1:3). Jesus calls the Holy Spirit "another encourager," thereby implying that he, too, was an encourager in his disciples' lives (John 14:16). If God was not an encourager, none of us would be able to go on serving him in such a discouraging world. Since, however, he is the "God of all encouragement," we have more than adequate resources to keep living for him. This secret enabled the early Christians to persevere with joy in spite of all the adversity they faced—they "went on. . . in the encouragement of the Holy Spirit" (Acts 9:31). They believed God was a God of encouragement and they knew how to receive his encouragement. When we receive God's encouragement and respond to it properly, he strengthens our spirits to play our parts in this battle with renewed vigor.

God is thus the ultimate source of spiritual encouragement for all Christians, even when this encouragement comes to us through each other. Paul alludes to this fact in 2 Corinthians 7:5,6. He says, "Even when we came into Macedonia our flesh had no rest, but we were afflicted on every side: conflicts without, fears within. But God, who encourages the depressed, encouraged us *by the coming of Titus.*" Although God can and does encourage us directly, he often chooses to communicate his encouragement to us through the agency of other Christians. This is what makes Christian encouragement something supernatural. As we express love to one another in this way, we become instruments of God's encouragement.

The Many Faces of Encouragement

Our lives are complex. We have a variety of fears and we face a variety of difficult situations. Because God is aware of this fact, he reveals several different "faces" of encouragement through his word.

Affirming Potential

Encouragement may involve *affirming another Christian's potential.* All of us struggle to some degree with thoughts and feelings of worthlessness. Some wrestle regularly with thoughts that they are "losers." Even the most confident people wrestle with such debilitating thoughts when they experience failure in important areas. God knows we never outgrow the need for this kind of encouragement. That's why he includes so much affirmation of our value and potential in his Word. And that's why he sends us to other Christians to express this affirmation.

John 1:42 records Peter's initial encounter with Jesus. "Jesus gazed intently at him, and said, 'You are Simon the son of John; you shall be called Cephas (which translated means Peter).'" Peter's original name was Simon, which was associated with the idea of "vacillator." What an accurate name this was for Peter! Throughout the gospels, Peter is the picture of instability. One minute he expresses amazing commitment to God and insight into spiritual things; the next minute he misses by a mile (see Matthew 16:15-23; John 13:6-10; Mark 14:27-72). Jesus clearly saw this flaw in Peter's character from the outset—but he also saw Peter's potential if he was submitted to God, motivated by Christ's love, and empowered by God's Spirit. This is what he communicated to Peter by saying "You *shall* be called Cephas." Cephas means "rock." The Vacillator would become known as the Rock as he followed Jesus. No wonder Peter committed his life to Jesus! This encouragement changed the course of Peter's life.

God has encouraged me in the same way through other Christians. As a new Christian, I had no vision whatever for my value and potential for God. Consequently, I had little motivation to grow spiritually and I struggled to make sense of what it meant to walk with Christ. God sent two older Christians to me who told me God had gifted me to communicate his Word to others. They saw my God-given potential that I couldn't see for myself, and they communicated a vision for my life at a critical time. I'm sure they have long forgotten their conversations with me, but over twenty years later, I still remember their words as if it was yesterday. Their encouragement motivated me to begin seriously pursuing God's will for my life. Ever since then, I have looked for opportunities to communicate this kind of encouragement to other younger Christians. Solomon says, "A man has joy in an apt answer, and how delightful is a timely word!" (Proverbs 15:23). It can be just as satisfying to be the sender of such encouragement as it is to be the receiver. Who are the Christians God wants you to encourage in this way?

Recognizing Spiritual Accomplishments

We can also communicate God's encouragement by *recognizing significant spiritual accomplishments*. Parents strengthen toddlers to keep trying until they learn to walk by praising their attempts. A recent survey reveals that the number one motivator of employees—outranking salary raises and working conditions—is recognition of work well done by their supervisors. This desire to hear someone say "Well done!" is instilled by God, and Christ will ultimately fulfill it in the next life when he rewards us for our service to him in this life (Matthew 25:21,23;

1 Corinthians 4:5). Of course, we can corrupt this desire so that we begin to live for the praise of certain people. Christians therefore need to learn how to persevere without such human recognition, trusting God to encourage them in other ways. When we receive recognition for godly accomplishments, and respond with humble gratitude to God, this can be a powerful and biblical incentive to go on living for him. Encouragement through recognition is therefore an important expression of love that all Christians should be able to effectively communicate.

Paul was a master at this kind of encouragement; it was a key feature of his dynamic leadership. In 1 Thessalonians 1:2-8, he pointed out to this struggling infant church the many ways they were living for God. He brought to their attention their "work of faith and labor of love and steadfastness of hope." He praised them for their evangelistic efforts, through which they had become "an example to all the believers in Macedonia and Achaia (because) the word of the Lord has sounded forth from you." He reminded them of how they "turned from idols to serve the living and true God." Paul knew the importance of this kind of positive feedback, and wherever it was appropriate he gave it in lavish portions.

New Christians thrive on this recognition as they are learning how to walk with Christ. They are often so aware of their biblical ignorance, of their awkwardness in prayer, of how far they have to go in spiritual growth that they don't see the significant progress they are making. They tend to compare themselves to older Christians in these areas and conclude they are hopelessly deficient. Meanwhile, older Christians are often uplifted to hear them pray or share in a group setting, or to learn of their willingness to share Christ with their friend, or to see their excitement about learning God's Word. Take the time to describe their progress and communicate how much it builds you up. You will be amazed at the impact this will often have.

We can also build up older Christians by recognizing their spiritual accomplishments. As we saw earlier, Timothy encouraged Paul by his report that the Corinthian Christians loved and appreciated him: ". . . but God, who strengthens the depressed, strengthened me by the coming of Titus, as he reported to us your longing, your mourning, your zeal for me; so that I rejoiced . . ." (2 Corinthians 7:7). Paul looked forward to visiting the Roman Christians "so that I may be encouraged together with you while among you, each of us by the other's faith, both yours and mine" (Romans 1:12). God will sometimes test your commitment to him by asking you to follow and serve him without such encouragement; but at other times he will also communicate his commitment to you through other Christians' gratitude for your ministry. God often prompts me to encourage other older Christians in this way. I often dismiss such promptings, thinking "She already knows that. I don't want her to get a big head." However, when I act on these promptings, I am often amazed to discover that this was exactly what the other person needed at that time. It's just as exciting to be on the giving end of this ministry as it is to be on the receiving end!

Communicating God's Faithfulness

You can also *communicate God's faithfulness to Christians who are hurting or fearful.* We live in a horribly abnormal world, and God does not spare us the pain of living in such a world. Loved ones die. Christian friends turn away from following Christ. God reveals new depths to our own sinfulness. Disappointment and failure mar our efforts to serve Christ. Agonizing conflicts go unresolved. You may not be able to explain why such things happen or feel their suffering as deeply as they do, but you can sensitively point them to the God who is perfect in his understanding and infinite in his compassion.

Paul reminded the Thessalonian Christians who had lost some of their friends to death that death is not the last word for those who have received Christ. After declaring to them that the dead in Christ will be raised at his return, Paul said "Therefore, encourage one another with these words" (1 Thessalonians 4:18). In the same letter, he urged them to "encourage the faint-hearted." "Faint-hearted" refers literally to those who are "small-souled." As we gently remind those who have had the spiritual wind knocked out of them of promises in God's word that pertain to their situations, God often uses their words to revive them.

Challenging At "Crunch Time"

We can also *challenge other Christians to go on following Christ despite their pain and fears.* Athletes know the importance of this kind of encouragement. When everything within them wants to give up, their coaches' challenges are often the margin between winning and losing. This is the main ingredient of the "home field advantage." Marathon runners who have "hit the wall" often get an extra surge of energy after they see a loved one cheering them on. Endurance and perseverance are necessary for those who want to win, and this kind of encouragement reminds us to stick it out.

Fearful, suffering Christians need more than consolation and reminders of God's faithfulness; they also need to be challenged to keep going despite their pain and fears. Paul encouraged the Philippian Christians by telling them, "For to you it has been granted for Christ's sake, not only to believe in him, but also to suffer for his sake" (Philippians 1:29). Sometimes I want pity, but I may need someone to warn me that my unfaithfulness will block God's healing power, and to challenge me to quit feeling sorry for myself and get back in the race. In a soft culture that has lost any idea of suffering for a cause bigger than ourselves, we often need reminders that it is our responsibility and privilege to suffer for the cause of Christ.

The recipients of the letter of Hebrews had been horribly persecuted in the past for their commitment to Christ, and similar persecution loomed again on the horizon. After reminding them of Christ's faithfulness to forgive their sins and help them overcome temptation, the author urges them to

> . . . Run with endurance the race that is set before us . . . you have not yet resisted to the point of shedding blood . . . strengthen the hands that are weak and the knees that are feeble, and make straight paths for your feet, so that the limb which is lame may not be put out of joint, but rather be healed. (Hebrews 12:1,4,12,13)

Many in our culture would view such encouragement as insensitive, but it was exactly what they needed. It is exactly what we often need as well.

Becoming an Effective Encourager

There is a spiritual gift of encouragement that some Christians possess while others do not. (Romans 12:8). These Christians seem to have an intuitive sense for who God wants them to encourage and how to express his encouragement. However, many passages urge *all* Christians to encourage one another. This must mean that, although we may not have this gift, encouragement is an expression of Christian love at which all of us can and should become effective. Here are some guidelines to help us progress toward this goal.

Receive God's Encouragement

If you want to become an effective encourager, you will need to *know how to receive God's encouragement in your own life.* Paul indicates that receiving God's encouragement enables us to encourage others. In 2 Corinthians 1:4, he says "[God] encourages us in all of our afflictions *so that* we may be able to encourage those who are in any affliction. . ." There are certain things we can do to receive God's encouragement. We should regularly ask him to encourage us. We should privately study and reflect on his Word, seeking for promises and other passages that strengthen and motivate us. We should regularly meet with other Christians to pray and study God's Word. The author of Hebrews singles out this activity as a uniquely rich environment for spiritual encouragement by saying ". . .not forsaking our own assembling together, as is the habit of some, but encouraging one another. . ." (Hebrews 10:24,24). Through the years, I have learned that the times when I least feel like going to such gatherings are the times when I most need to go. When the Bible seems to be dead and when prayer seems impossible, God's encouragement gets through to me in the environment of Christian fellowship.

Christian workers also need to be willing to ask for help when they become chronically discouraged. We may think, "I don't want to take their valuable time, I'll work it out myself." Of course, it may sometimes be preferable to do this. At other times, though, this statement betrays a prideful determination to work our way out of discouragement without the help of other Christians. There is no profit in playing hero if it takes us out of the battle! It is not a luxury to ask for help when we are fainting; it is a responsibility so we can remain at our posts and be effective.

Trust God to Encourage You in His Way and Timing

While some Christians are reluctant to ask for encouragement even when they need it, others are quick to demand it. For this reason, it is also important to *trust God to encourage you in the way and in the timing he chooses.* Many Christians become embittered toward God or others because he will not comply with their demands to encourage them immediately, through the people they choose, or in the way they want. We will be disappointed if we make such demands on God and threaten to go on strike unless he comes through for us in this way.

This attitude expresses unbelief in God's goodness and will only short-circuit our ability to receive his encouragement. God knows best how and when to encourage us, and no amount of pressure on our part will force his hand. Instead, we need to ask God to encourage us, and put ourselves in the scripturally defined environment for encouragement. Then we should express our trust that God will encourage us by continuing to follow and serve him. God's encouragement is "effective in the patient enduring of (our) sufferings . . ." (2 Corinthians 1:6). As we determine to patiently endure difficulty while remaining at our posts, God will prove his faithfulness to encourage us.

Use God's Word

Since God is the source of spiritual encouragement, *knowing and using God's Word* is a key for those who effectively encourage others. Paul says elders must have a good grasp of God's Word "that they may encourage others in sound doctrine" (Titus 1:9). This doesn't mean that we merely quote scripture to people and send them on their way! This is not encouragement; it is condescension. Rather, we can explain relevant scriptures and discuss their application. We can share how God has encouraged us through passages of scripture. We can lead people through questions to remember what they already know of God's Word. There are many creative ways of using scripture in encouragement, but it is central in this ministry. Ultimately, we must do more than just listen and express empathy. This may be of some help, but it is ultimately inadequate unless we point people to what God says. It is God's Word that sets people free by giving them the insight they need and by challenging them to trust him in practical ways.

Consider How to Stimulate

The author of Hebrews urges us to "*consider* how to stimulate one another to love and good deeds . . . encouraging one another . . ." (Hebrews 10:24,25). For most of us, effective encouragement is seldom an intuitive, spontaneous event. It usually requires careful and prayerful forethought. If we want to be effective encouragers when present with people, we will need to reflect on such things when absent from them. This is often the key to the atmosphere of Christian meetings. Some meetings are so dead they feel like a funeral parlor. Others have a sense of electric anticipation in the air. Since God's Spirit is equally present in both meetings, what is the reason for this difference? The key, I believe, is not the leaders or the teacher, though these people can exert strong spiritual influence on the meeting. It usually depends more on the proportion of those present who have sacrificially prepared themselves in advance through such prayerful consideration. They have come ready to encourage others, sometimes even though they themselves bear great burdens. The more we do this, the more avenues the Lord has to lift up those who are present, and the more the atmosphere is charged with a sense of spiritual anticipation.

Learn the Art of Listening

Effective encouragers are usually *good listeners*. They ask other Christians about their spiritual lives because of genuinely interest, and they pay careful attention to the answers they get. The better we are at prayerfully listening to people, the more we will be able to discern what kind of encouragement they need. Careful listening tends to make others more receptive to our encouragement when we offer it, because our listening has demonstrated love and respect. Sadly, many are essentially self-centered in their conversations with other Christians, capable of communicating only superficial interest in others because they don't care about others or only want to talk about themselves. Other-centered listening is a discipline that takes practice, but it will pay big dividends if we want to influence others spiritually.

Practice, Practice, Practice!

Effectiveness in encouragement, like proficiency in any area of spiritual ministry, takes *practice*. This is especially important to remember if we feel awkward in encouraging others. If we wait until we feel "natural" doing this, we will still be waiting when Christ returns! Though there may be many reasons for feelings of awkwardness in encouragement, practicing is essential if we want to eventually feel more natural in doing it. Furthermore, God will greatly use even our awkward attempts at encouragement when we are sincere. Look for the opportunities that God gives you daily to encourage others. Don't wait for others to take the lead in encouragement. Be a leader through your own example.

Discussion Questions

1. Share specific incidents when God encouraged you through other Christians. What biblical truths were communicated? How were they communicated effectively? What difference did it make?

2. Which forms of encouragement come easiest to you? What opportunities currently exist for you to give this form of encouragement?

3. Which forms of encouragement are most difficult for you? What opportunities currently exist for you to give this form of encouragement?

5

Admonish One Another

Let the word of Christ dwell in you richly as you teach and
admonish one another with all wisdom. . .
Colossians 3:16

Biblical admonition is moral correction through verbal confrontation motivated by genuine concern. The Greek word most often translated "admonish," *noutheteo*, means "to place upon one's mind." Words like "rebuke," "reprove," "correct," and "warn" are all synonyms of "admonish." God admonishes us because he cares about us, and because he knows we are damaging ourselves and others through wrong attitudes and actions. He admonishes us directly through his Word, but he also admonishes us through other Christians—and he calls each of us to a ministry of admonition.

Admonition is the complement of encouragement. Encouragement is grounded in the biblical assumption that we are fearful people who need God's support; admonition is grounded in the biblical assumption that we are sinful people who need God's moral correction. Encouragement supports people by urging them to respond to God's gracious promises; admonition corrects people by calling on them to respond to God's moral will. Both are expressions of biblical love, which gives others what they need according to a biblical understanding of people. Because Jesus loved Peter, he both encouraged him by affirming his potential ("You shall be called 'rock'") and rebuked him for his self-centeredness ("Get behind me . . . for you are not setting your mind on God's interests, but on man's").

Although these two forms of biblical love balance and temper one another, they are often pitted against one another. Our culture has largely rejected the legitimacy of moral absolutes and therefore equates moral correction with unloving intolerance. According to today's secular climate, we are capable of healthy moral self-direction and external moral correction renders us dysfunctional. Admonition is therefore unnecessary and even harmful. Unfortunately, many Christians have assimilated this mentality to a remarkable degree. They view encouragement as mandatory to spiritual growth, but admonition is tragically absent from their view of love. It is not "politically correct" in the current climate for Christians to confront one another about moral issues. Those who admonish other Christians run the risk of being called intrusive at best, and spiritually abusive at worst. Yet the New Testament is clear that it is not possible to love one another without admonishing one another.

Since admonition is an aspect of biblical love, all Christians have the responsibility to admonish. Church leaders have a special responsibility to admonish those under their charge. Accordingly, approximately half of the New Testament passages concerning admonition addressed leaders. Leaders must be willing to supply moral correction even when this is unpopular. Other passages, however, address all Christians, which makes it clear that reciprocal admonition is a mandatory aspect of Christian community. Two passages are particularly clear on this. In Romans 15:14, Paul said "I. . . am convinced that you. . . are full of goodness, filled with all knowledge, and able also to admonish one another." Even though Paul had never visited the Roman Christians and knew none of them personally, he expressed his confidence that they were capable of mutual admonition. Why? Because they possessed goodness, which means loving concern for one another's well-being—and because they possessed knowledge, which refers to their access to God's Word. Any Christian who cares about his friends and knows what the Bible says is qualified, according to Paul, to admonish.

Paul repeats this conviction in Colossians 3:16, where he calls on all the Christians in that local church to "Be filled the word of Christ, teaching and admonishing one another with all wisdom. . .." Again, even though he knew none of these people, Paul expressed confidence that every Colossian Christian possessed the resources for effective admonition. As they looked to God's word and employed wisdom in their dealings with each other, they could instruct and correct each other in ways that would promote spiritual maturity.

Receiving Admonition

Since admonition should be reciprocal in the church ("admonish *one another*"), we should become effective both in receiving it and in giving it.

Like other forms of God's discipline, admonition "seems not to be joyful, but sorrowful; yet for those who are trained by it, afterwards it yields the peaceful fruit of righteousness" (Hebrews 12:11). No one really enjoys being corrected for moral wrongs. On one level, this is simply because admonition is painful, and we shouldn't enjoy pain! Since all of us need admonition from time to time, though, we might as well learn how to get the most out of it.

Aversion to Admonition

Admonition can be especially painful for those who have experienced a pattern of personal rejection along with correction by key authority figures. If our childhood authority figures used correction without genuine loving concern or as a means of retribution, we can develop a reflex negative response to all correction. This is understandable, but it is certainly not necessary for us to go on viewing all admonition this way. That *some* people replace correction with rejection does not mean *all* correction is rejection. Indeed, unless we learn to differentiate godly admonition from rejection, we won't be able to mature spiritually because "God disciplines us that we may share his holiness" (Hebrews 12:10). This is why it is important to understand God's grace if we want to profit from admonition. God never rejects his children, and he always disciplines us in love. The better we understand this and the more we believe it, the easier it will be to interpret admonition as an act of love and profit from it instead of interpreting it as proof of rejection and reacting against it.

It would be a mistake, however, to blame all negative reactions to admonition on past abuse. Even those who have not experienced serious abuse of admonition normally have a negative initial response to it. This is because, as fallen people, we have an ingrained tendency to rebel against God's authority and insist on our own way. When other Christians correct us, even in a careful and loving way, we normally experience something within us that rises up in outrage. Our rage naturally focuses on minor flaws in the admonisher and we use these flaws as an excuse to ignore its content. "How dare she raise her voice to me!" "He should have tried to encourage me more!" "Where does he get off telling me about my sins when he has plenty of his own?" Some even reject correction on the grounds that "You hurt my feelings when you said that!"

Certainly, this statement reveals profound immaturity. The issue, after all, is not whether our feelings were hurt; it is whether the admonition was accurate. Maturing Christians know their depravity and are deeply suspicious of the tendency to react negatively to admonition. As long as we reserve the right to reject admonition unless others give it in a perfect or painless way, we will remain at a very primitive state of spiritual development. Wisdom and maturity come to those who learn to view correction as a means of God's love and respond properly to it. This is a major theme in Solomon's writings:

> "Whoever loves discipline loves knowledge, but he who hates discipline is stupid" (Proverbs 12:1).

> "He who neglects discipline despises himself, but he who listens to reproof acquires understanding" (Proverbs 15:32,33).

> "A man who hardens his neck after much reproof will suddenly be broken beyond remedy" (Proverbs 29:1).

> "It is better to listen to the rebuke of a wise man than for one to listen to the song of fools" (Ecclesiastes 7:5).

Focusing On the Content of the Admonition

It is important, then, to look for the truth in correction rather than looking for the excuses to reject it. Admonition is a labor of love. Few people in our lives will care about us enough to risk giving us this kind of help. Fewer still will take this risk again if we respond defensively or counter-attack. When we are admonished, we should ask ourselves two questions: "Do I recognize this attitude or action in my life?" and "Does the Bible speak of this as morally wrong?" If the answer to these questions is "yes," we should thank our friend for bringing this to our attention, and then set about changing our ways with God's help. Often, the validity of the correction is apparent to us immediately or even before someone corrects us. Because we are all prone to self-righteousness and self-deception, though, we may need to prayerfully consider the content of the admonition before we can see how it fits.

Of course, there may be times when we conclude an admonition is not accurate. When this is the case, we should reject it, or at least ask for more clarification. Some Christians have over-sensitive consciences and confess to virtually every sin charged to them. Some want acceptance from other people so badly that they acknowledge and apologize even for things of which they do not believe they are guilty. However, it is just as wrong to apologize for what we do not believe is wrong as it is to refuse to apologize for what we know is wrong. Unfortunately, some Christians have a personal ax to grind, and accuse others falsely. Others keep their own guilty consciences at bay by nit-picking and accusing others. The Corinthian Christians were apparently engaging in this kind of blame-shifting when they accused Paul of doing Christian ministry from wrong motives. Paul denied that he was guilty of this sin, and he called on them to desist from their accusations (1 Corinthians 4:3-5).

What is the pattern in your own life? Do you tend to respond to correction defensively? Do you tend to just agree and apologize immediately whether you are guilty or not? Have you taught people not to bother correcting you because they will have to endure a terrible counterattack? Or have you learned Solomon's insight: "Faithful are the wounds of a friend" (Prov. 27:6)?

Giving Admonition

To Admonish or Not to Admonish

Because of the complexity of human situations, it is impossible to prescribe a formula for when admonition is appropriate. Jesus said, "When your brother sins, go and reprove him" (Matthew 18:15). However, he gave us valuable guidance by sandwiching this statement between two parables. In the preceding context, he told the parable of the shepherd who left the ninety-nine sheep to find the one sheep who was lost. In the following context, Jesus told the parable of the forgiven steward who refused to forgive his debtor. Before admonishing someone, therefore, it is important to prayerfully ask ourselves: "Have I forgiven the other person for the hurt he caused me, or do I want to pay him back?" "Am I honestly committed to seeking his good, or am I more interested in venting my own anger because I was offended?" Unless we can answer these questions affirmatively, we cannot trust our judgment about whether and how to admonish.

Additional questions can help us to decide whether admonition is appropriate and how to communicate it. Does the Bible clearly describe this issue as sin?

Do you know that the person did what you think? If this is unclear, we may still decide to talk to the other person, but it is wise to ask questions or raise concerns rather than delivering a rebuke. We should be especially careful about judging the motives of others when their actions are not clearly wrong. Motivation is a moral issue, but we are not equipped to detect wrong motivation as accurately as we can detect wrong behavior. Is the person already aware of this issue and working on it? If this is the case, perhaps our best response is usually to show patience and forbearance. Wisdom dictates that we should know our own temperamental tendencies. Do you tend to be excessively critical or excessively soft in your dealings with others? If so, you may need to check yourself to see whether you arc chickening out of giving a needed admonition. If, however, you tend to be overly critical in your dealings with others, you may need to ask yourself why you shouldn't practice forbearance.

Other Christians can often help us discern whether admonition is necessary and how to give it. Especially if they have experience in Christian ministry, or if they know us and the persons involved, they are God's resource for helping us in this important labor of love. Though this resource can be abused by gossip, it is unscriptural to think we should not confer with other Christians in this way.[1]

An Encouraging Context

Others will more readily receive admonition when we give it in an environment of encouragement. Both common sense and personal experience teach us that we are more open to receive correction from those who have expressed affirmation and belief in us. Encouragement tends to help us make the distinction between what we do (which is the subject of admonition) and who we are. In this environment, people more easily perceive admonition as the loving action that it is. In a healthy family, for example, parents build an encouragement-rich environment that provides a context for their children to benefit most from their parents' admonition.

This principle, however, does not prevent us from admonishing people unless we know them well and have been giving them lots of encouragement recently. This erroneous conclusion is implied by the maxim that we must "earn the right to be heard." Admonition is not a right that we earn; it is grace that we give and a labor of love. We should build an encouraging relationship whenever possible, but situations sometimes arise in which we must take action without this preparation. Sometimes those who are closest to an errant Christian are unwilling to admonish him, and it falls to others to do this. Sometimes the errant Christian has rejected the admonition of those closest to him, so others must confirm the seriousness of the problem (Matt. 18:15-16). Sometimes the wrong is so flagrant that it requires an immediate and strong admonition.

Another qualification to this principle is necessary. We should not necessarily conclude that we shouldn't have admonished someone, or that we admonished him wrongly just because he responded poorly. Because we are sinful and can harden our hearts against correction, people can and do reject admonition even when others give it with loving motivation and in an appropriate way. Parents, for example, know that their children frequently react to some discipline with the charge that it was unfair or unloving. Unless we have a category in our own minds for this, we will tend to evaluate the legitimacy of our admonition on the person's response rather than on the basis that we did it in a biblical way.

In Private and Face to Face

Jesus said, "When you brother sins, go and reprove him in private" (Matthew 18:15). In most cases, we should admonish in private. Though it may be more convenient or less scary for us to correct someone in the presence of others, it usually not best for the person we are correcting. This is because private admonition makes it easier for the other person to listen to our correction without being defensive. We should reserve group or public admonition for serious sins or for when the person has demonstrated an unwillingness to respond to earlier private admonition.

Likewise, a face-to-face setting is preferable to a phone call or a letter. Of course, there are exceptions to this, but this is a rule of thumb. We may feel more comfortable confronting someone with the protection afforded by a phone or a letter, but the goal is to help the other person—not to make it easy for us. Much communication is nonverbal, and only face-to-face conversation allows full nonverbal communication. There may be issues that we need to discuss or clarify on the spot, and this is not possible in a letter. A face-to-face meeting communicates both directness and vulnerability from the one who is admonishing.

Be Direct and Specific

Get right to the point. Long introductions or encouraging statements are usually unhelpful because they can be confusing. The other person usually senses something is up and wants to know what it is. Most times, we are reluctant to get to the point because of our fears rather than because of redemptive concern for the other person. The tension is already there, and the best way to break it is to state our concern.

Vague, general admonitions are also unhelpful. If we open the conversation by saying, "Your attitude has been lousy lately," we can expect confusion or resistance. Conversely, "You lost your temper and spoke abusively to Mike this morning" is specific enough to immediately focus the issue.

In some cases, we may need to surface the issue with a question. "I noticed last week you didn't come home on two nights. Did you spend those nights at your girlfriend's house?" Depending on the person's answer, we will have to decide how to pursue the issue, but we have cleared the air by surfacing the issue in a direct manner.

Appeal to Scripture

Christian admonition should appeal to the Bible as the moral authority. We are not confronting the other person because she rubbed us the wrong way, or because we have decided to be her ultimate judge, but because she has violated God's moral will. We are coming to her as a fellow Christian, equally under God's moral authority ourselves, calling her to the same accountability to God to which we ourselves submit. We should make it clear that the primary issue is not between us and the other person, but rather between her and God. We can simply state this, or we can show where the Bible speaks to the issue.

Because the Bible is God's Word, it has the power to convict people of sin in ways that are impossible for us. If we forget this, we may tend to resort to our own cleverness or our charm or the forcefulness of our personalities. Instead, we should rely on the power of God's truth and the convicting work of his Spirit. Remember "the Word of God is living and active, sharper than any two-edged sword, piercing as far as the division between soul and spirit... able to judge the thoughts and intentions of the heart" (Hebrews 4:12).

Be Patient Rather Than Insisting On Immediate Response

To give God the opportunity to convict the other person, we should normally urge him to prayerfully reflect on what we have said if he doesn't respond properly to our admonition. Unless the matter is so serious that immediate compliance is necessary (physical violence, for example), it is usually best to respond to his resistance by saying, "I'd like you to think and pray about what I've shared with you on this issue. Let's talk more about this in a couple of days." This gives the person some time to calm down, and it affords God some time to penetrate his initial resistance with his conviction. Of course, it is important to follow up such a suggestion by revisiting the issue soon. No doubt this is why Jesus prescribed multiple discussions in Matthew 18:15-17.

Be Constructive When Possible

Galatians 6:2 says we should "restore" those who have been caught in any trespass. This verse certainly underscores the importance of having a redemptive attitude toward the people we admonish, but it also urges us to go even farther. Are there practical ways in which we can help the person overcome this sin? Is there additional help we might be able to give? It is certainly valid to say, "God says you should not be having sex with your girlfriend." After the person has agreed that this is wrong, however, it may be more helpful to follow this admonition with a suggestion: "Why don't you and your girlfriend evaluate what situations make it easy for you to fall sexually, and agree together to avoid those situations?" Being constructive may require mental effort on our part before we admonish someone, but such effort is part of being a restorative influence.

There are times when we must address issues without having any constructive practical help to offer. If we have made the effort and come up empty, we often still need to be willing to speak the corrective word. In these situations, it is sufficient to say that we would like to be able to help more, and that we will be praying for God to give the person the insight he may need to overcome this issue. We may also urge him to talk to someone who may be able to give him this kind of help.

End With Encouragement When Appropriate

What if the other person responds to our admonition with humility and agreement about the need to change? In most cases, our response should be to encourage him. The prodigal son's father rejoiced and embraced his son upon his return (Luke 15:20). Paul urged the Corinthians to reaffirm their love for an errant brother who had repented (2 Cor. 2:8). Find a way to express your personal satisfaction with his response and your anticipation that it will result in further spiritual growth.

Sometimes people show a pattern of responding to admonition positively in a verbal way while continuing to demonstrate a lack of repentance in their actions. When this is the case, it usually best to withhold encouragement until a change of behavior is evident. Then the encouragement will reinforce real repentance and not mere verbal agreement.

Admonition and Encouragement Set the Tone in Christian Community

Admonition and encouragement are crucial factors in the tone of a Christian community, whether it be a small group, a whole church, or a Christian family. Consider each quadrant of the following chart as representing a Christian community. What kind of tone would exist in each group?

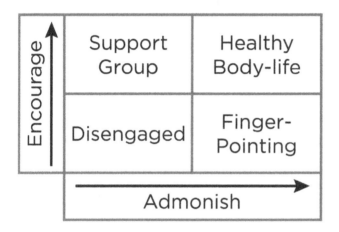

Many Christian groups are low in both encouragement and admonition. This is the "disengaged" group, which is not a community at all. People are not involved with each other on a personal level. In such groups, a silent consensus usually forms that the members do not share their fears or admit their moral problems. Instead, they tend to posture that "everything is fine with me" regardless of what is going on spiritually. While this kind of group demands little risk or account-ability, it also provides little real direction, support, or intimacy. It is superficial.

Many Christian groups are high in encouragement but low in admonition. We could call this the "support group." Our society often characterizes such groups as loving. The atmosphere of the group tends to be affirming and nurturing, but it lacks moral fiber. In this environment, people feel affirmed while their problems go unaddressed and often get worse. Those who are willing to admonish often grow frustrated because they sense that others will not back them up when they take a confrontational stand. Admonition may even be frowned upon as unloving–but encouragement without appropriate admonition creates a flabby group that does not promote spiritual growth.

Christian groups that are high in admonition but low in encouragement tend to develop a harsh or even self-righteous tone. In this "finger-pointing" atmosphere, members address one another's moral problems promptly and strongly, but a climate of fear develops because they don't regularly remind each other of God's faithfulness. Anger rather than love often becomes the central motive for admonition. In this environment, people tend to retreat from personal vulnerability, posture the externals of Christian living, and focus more on other's sins than on their own spiritual growth.

God's ideal is a Christian community in which the members encourage one another regularly and admonish each other as needed. This is not to imply that we should give encouragement and admonition equal amounts. Healthy groups (and friendships and families) express more encouragement than admonition. The point is that we are willing to admonish whenever it is needed, and we do it for the good of the loved ones. In other words, we "speak the truth to one another in love" (Ephesians 4:15). This is the group that follows Paul's advice to the Thessalonians: "Admonish the unruly, encourage the fainthearted . . . be patient with everybody" (1 Thessalonians 5:14). The result, according to Paul, is not a perfect community, but "the growth of the body for the building up of itself in love" (Ephesians 4:16).

Discussion Questions

1. Share specific incidents when God admonished you through other Christians. What impact did this admonition have on your spiritual life? When was the last time another Christian admonished you? What was the result?

2. Using the chart at the end of the chapter, how would you describe your own involvement with other Christians friends? What steps can you take toward more healthy involvement?

3. Using the chart at the end of the chapter, how would you describe your church? What could help it move toward becoming a more healthy community?

6

Confess Your Sins to One Another

. . .confess your sins to one another, and pray for one another, so that you may be healed.
James 5:16

Confession dredges up all sorts of uncomfortable images for many of us—yet God has included it as one of the keys to healthy love relationships. James says, "confess your sins to one another" (James 5:16).

What is Confession?

The New Testament word for "confess" is *homolego*, which means literally "say with" or "agree with." When we confess our sins to one another, we say the same thing God says about them—we take responsibility for them as sins rather than rationalizing them or blaming them on other people or circumstances. Sometimes we need to confess our sins to people against whom we have sinned to be reconciled to them. Sometimes we need to confess our sins to other Christian friends to seek their help to overcome these sins.

Confusion About Confession

To profit from confession, we first need to clear away our misconceptions concerning this practice. Confession is a complex issue, so it is liable to confusion and misconception. Then too, we have different religious backgrounds and temperamental tendencies—and these can create very different problems with confession.

Necessary for God's Forgiveness?

Some people view confession to other people as something necessary to get God's forgiveness. According to Roman Catholic doctrine, for example, the priest has divine authority to dispense God's forgiveness through the sacraments of confession and penance.[1] Unless you are willing to confess your sins to a priest and follow his instructions on doing penance, God's forgiveness will not be dispensed to you. Such teaching, however, is a direct contradiction to the New Testament, which insists that God declares us righteous solely through our faith in Christ, apart from any other human mediator (Gal. 2:16; 1 Tim. 2:5). Because our acceptance by God is based entirely on Christ's finished work, we may come into God's presence at any time with full assurance that he accepts us (Heb. 10:19-22).

Throwing the Baby Out With the Bath Water

Christians who have learned the liberating power of God's complete forgiveness sometimes react against their experiences with confession to the point of denying that it has any value in the Christian life. This is throwing the baby out with the bath water. Confession to other Christians is in no way necessary for God's forgiveness, but it still has an important role to play. Actually, knowing that God has completely forgiven us should free us to be open about our sins with God and others. Since God has forever removed the threat of his rejection, we can afford to be honest with others about our moral struggles. This grace-based honesty is an important feature of spiritual growth and quality relationships, as we shall soon see.

I Already Confessed to God

Some Christians conclude that as long as they confess their sins to God, they need not confess their sins to other people. This brings up a confusing issue, because we need not confess all sins to others. We'll look at this issue more closely later, but clearly we must confess some sins to others before they can be effectively resolved. For example, people who have been sexually unfaithful to their spouses should normally confess this and ask for their forgiveness. This is important for two reasons. First, they made a vow to their spouses to remain faithful to them, and they have broken that vow. They owe it to their spouses to tell them.

Second, they cannot restore their relationship's lost intimacy until they divulge this information. They will continue to wonder how their spouse would react if they knew of their unfaithfulness, and this lack of resolution will prevent the relationship from being genuinely healed. In reality, this fear of confession is usually an attempt to avoid the full consequences of adultery. Those who oppose this position usually say, "I have confessed it to God. I don't need to confess to anyone else." The truth is that until they confess it to their spouses, they are adversely affecting their relationship with both their spouse and God.

Confession to Avoid Repentance

Some Christians misuse confession as a way of avoiding real repentance—the choice to change our attitude and direction. Children often employ this tactic with their parents. When caught, they may tearfully cry, "I'm sorry!" not because they have repented, but to avoid disciplinary consequences. Sadly, many of us never outgrow this dangerous practice. Some Christians are adept at discerning when others plan to admonish them. They then initiate an apology, but their motive is to get people off their backs so they can go on doing what they want to do. At best, this is purposeful hypocrisy and manipulation. At worst, it can become a dangerous form of self-deception by which we convince ourselves that we are repentant when we are not. In this way, we can pervert confession into a means of perpetuating our sinful habits instead of employing it as a means of liberation from them.

Saul, Israel's first king, demonstrated this misuse of confession on several occasions. When Samuel confronted him with his disobedience to God's command to destroy the Amalekites, Saul first insisted that he had obeyed the Lord. When Samuel persisted, Saul blamed his sin on the people. Finally, after Samuel declared that God had rejected him as king for his insubordination, Saul suddenly cried, "I have sinned. I violated the Lord's command and your instructions. I was afraid of the people and so I gave in to them" (1 Samuel 15:24 NIV). Sounds like a clean confession, doesn't it? The subsequent narrative, however, makes it clear that Saul was only trying to avoid the loss of his kingship. Throughout the rest of his forlorn reign, he verbalized apparently sincere confessions, only to continue down his chosen path of rebellion against God.

To Professionals Only

Many Christians understand that confession to other Christians is valid and even important, but they believe they should confess only to qualified, professional Christians. Today, with the rise of popularity in professional Christian counseling, many Christians feel they should confide their sins only in this context. This mentality represents conformity to our secular culture, which has relegated this kind of personal vulnerability to therapeutic experts. Reacting against this development, some Christian leaders are calling for people to return to their pastors for this kind of help. But this call only reaffirms the same "expert" mentality—this time in the form of a clergy-laity division. In reality, while both professional counselors and pastors can be helpful, confession to them is neither sufficient nor fully biblical. James says, "confess your sins to each other" (James 5:16). Paul likewise calls for us to "put off falsehood and speak truthfully to his neighbor" (Ephesians 4:25 NIV). Counselors and pastors can be a valuable supplement to authentic Christian community, but they can never replace it. Many problems confessed in the privacy of the counselor's (or pastor's) office could be more quickly and effectively resolved if they were confessed to close Christian friends. Many more problems would be nipped in the bud if Christians were more open with one another about their sins.

The Benefits of Confession

Most people view confession as a practice that somehow benefits God—but nothing could be further from the truth! God already knows what we have done, and he already accepts us in spite of our sins because of Christ's finished work. God surely enjoys our honesty with him, but he prescribes confession primarily for our benefit. When we relate honestly to God because we are confident of his acceptance, confession to other Christians becomes a crucial source of spiritual help.

Experiencing God's Forgiveness

God permanently forgives us once we receive Christ. He forever cancels our true moral guilt—past, present, and future—by Christ's payment on the cross (Colossians 2:13-14). However, our experiential assurance of that forgiveness is not constant; we must appropriate it on an ongoing basis. While there are no additional conditions for receiving God's objective forgiveness, there are sometimes additional conditions for experiencing it.

In many cases, we are able to experientially appropriate God's forgiveness by acknowledging to him that we have sinned, agreeing to return to his way in this area, and thanking him for his grace. Sometimes, however, we are unable to experience God's forgiveness until we also confess to others. Maybe it is because we have sinned against that person and need to resolve it with him. Maybe it is because we have betrayed a trust of our role in God's work, and integrity requires that we disclose this. Maybe it is because God wants us to practice openness and vulnerability with others. Maybe it is because God wants to liberate us from our dependence on other people's acceptance by risking rejection from them through confession. Maybe it is because God has decided to communicate the experiential (not judicial) sense of his forgiveness through other Christians so that we will learn a healthy dependence on them.

Several years ago, I traveled to the West Coast to attend a Christian conference. I went as a leader of our church to gather information for use in equipping other young Christians. While I was there, I fell to temptation and got high—an old habit from which God freed me shortly after I came to Christ. I did this only once, and I confessed it to God and thanked him for his forgiveness. Having done this, I tried to go on with my life as normal, but I couldn't shake a nagging sense of unresolved guilt. For a couple of days I agonized over this, telling myself that I was giving in to satanic accusation, that it was no big deal, that I had already confessed this matter to God and repented of it. I remembered a time when as a new Christian I had fallen in the same way. I had privately confessed it to God and immediately experienced his forgiveness that cleansed my conscience. Shouldn't I be able to do the same thing now? There was no relief until I confessed it to my wife and my fellow leaders. Only then was I able to be at peace with God on this matter and successfully put it behind me.

Why did God require me to confess this fall to others? I believe the main reason was that with higher levels of leadership in God's work comes greater account-ability for our moral lives. I had betrayed a trust as a leader of my church. I needed to disclose this betrayal and subject myself to their discipline. I also needed to humble myself to my wife by acknowledging this moral fall. What had been adequate for me as a new Christian was not sufficient for me as a Christian leader. I learned many valuable lessons from that experience, and one of them was the liberating power of confession to others.

Activating God's Empowering for Moral Change

Sin thrives in secrecy and darkness. The more we keep sin to ourselves, the more it deceives us and brings us under its power. Conversely, bringing sin out into the open weakens its power over us. Perhaps this is why James tells us to "confess your sins to each other and pray for each other so that you may be healed" (James 5:16 NIV).[2] As we choose to tell one another about our moral failures, and as we pray for one another in these areas, God is able to transform our characters more rapidly and more deeply than if we try to grow by ourselves. Because we are living in the light, God's Spirit is more free to empower us and work through us to affect others. The result is a much stronger impact for Christ on our society.

At the heart of the Wesleyan movement in the 1700s was the "band." These bands were small groups of Christians who met together weekly for the express purpose of practicing James 5:16.[3] John Wesley knew that the spiritual vitality of these new converts was sure to wane unless they practiced this kind of loving and prayerful accountability with one another. During the time when these bands were a central feature of Wesleyanism, the changed lives influenced the society and affected a nationwide spiritual renewal. Conversely, the curtailment of this structure was arguably the single biggest cause for Wesleyanism's gradual spiritual decline.

Creating an Environment for Healthy Corporate Life

In Ephesians 4:25, Paul says "each of you must put off falsehood and speak truthfully to his neighbor" (NIV). This verse is not a mere prohibition against telling lies to one another. It is fundamentally a call for Christians to relate to one another with true openness about their lives. Christians, of all people, should be able to be honest with one another about their sins and weaknesses because God, who knows all of their problems, has accepted them. As those who have discovered what it means to relate to God under grace, we have a basis for relating to each other under grace as well. Tragically, Christians are often more phony around each other than non-Christians. It is common to discover Christians who have been deeply defeated for months or years, yet none of their Christian friends knew about it because they were acting as if everything was fine. Religious phoniness, a form of hypocrisy, is a "leaven" (Luke 12:1) that easily infects and destroys the love relationships Jesus wants Christians to experience. No wonder Paul reminded the Ephesian Christians to avoid this like the plague!

We may say we relate in this phony way because we are afraid of what our Christian friends might do if we were honest. This is a lame excuse. The Lord has told us to lay aside the phoniness and speak the truth. If our friends reject us, we should pity them for their weakness, but we will still have Christ to uphold us. More likely, though, they will respond with mercy and try to help us. They may also be more open about their own struggles after seeing our example.

Why should Christians practice this kind of vulnerability with one another? Paul gives us his reason: "because we are members of one another." He refers to the spiritual union between Christians. "So in Christ we who are many form one body, and each member belongs to all the others" (Romans 12:5 NIV). When the members of our physical bodies are injured, they let the rest of the body know. The other members of our physical bodies contribute in various ways to the injured member's restoration. If my arm has an infection, it alerts the rest of my body to its condition. One member manufactures white blood cells to combat the infection; other members help those white cells to get to the site of the infection. My wound heals because the wound became a corporate issue. The same way of life applies to the Christian community because we are members of the same body through our union with Christ. As a suffering member, I am responsible to let the other members know and to allow them to help me as best they can (while continuing to seek help directly from the Lord as well). The Lord responds to my request by helping me directly, and by sending help indirectly through other Christians. However, his help is predicated on our willingness to ask for it by being open about our struggles.

Over the years, I have observed a clear correlation between the spiritual vitality in a Christian group and the level of its members' openness with each other about their sins and weaknesses. In some groups, there is a refreshing openness between the members in this area. People not only share past problems; they also divulge their current struggles. They inquire sensitively yet freely about one another's spiritual state. People give each other the freedom to ask about areas of temptation, and they thank their friends for taking advantage of this freedom. While they don't take gossip lightly, neither do they insist on strict confidentiality about their problems because they have a basic trust that the other members have their welfare in mind.[4] They even remind each other lovingly about their sinful tendencies!

Someone may say, "Lighten up, Bill. You're getting rigid with people again." You may hear someone else say, "You know you tend to run from conflict, so don't chicken out on confronting Sharon." The result is a refreshing and powerful sense of honesty and spiritual reality that helps Christians to grow. This kind of community also attracts non-Christians who are looking for healthy relationships. Of course, those who don't want spiritual authenticity and real change usually find this environment threatening. Ironically, non-Christians often love it, while many who have been Christians for years often flee from it as if it is a choking gas.

In other groups, one can sense that people are being false with one another. They hold each other at arm's length, courteous perhaps, but unwilling to admit their problems. Sins remain hidden until they are so big they are undeniable, and then people often leave because of the humiliation of exposure. Members don't know how to respond when someone is honest. There is embarrassment and awkwardness that effectively teaches people to act as if everything is fine. People take offense if you bring up their sinful tendencies or ask how they are doing in those areas. You get the impression that people are playing a game—and this is exactly what is happening. Those who want help quickly learn not to be honest about their problems, but to act as if they have it together and try to figure out on their own how to overcome their struggles.

Practical Guidelines

When to Confess to Others

There is no clear-cut scriptural answer to this question, but there are some principles we can follow. When we have wronged someone directly, we should usually acknowledge this wrong to them. We can usually resolve minor matters, like being late, by a simple apology. Serious offenses, such as theft or dishonesty, may require extensive disclosure and a request for forgiveness. It is not that greater sins require greater payment—this is a legalistic way of relating to one another. Rather, love dictates that we acknowledge the harmful impact that our wrong decisions have on others. Many of us have a highly developed sensitivity to others' sins against us, but we have little awareness of how our actions are affecting others. This is an immature perspective, and God wants to change us so that we become more sensitive to how we are affecting others and less sensitive to how they are affecting us. When we respond to God's conviction by confessing and apologizing for our sins, we free the Holy Spirit to mature us in this crucial area.

When we lack the insight or ability to get free from some sin, it is wise to seek help from another Christian. Recently, a good friend confided to me that he had been slowly wilting under a barrage of sexual temptation. In spite of his resistance, he had been giving way more and more to fantasies, and recently resumed an old pornography habit. He had initially resisted this temptation by trying to turn away from such thoughts. When he looked at a pornographic magazine, he appropriated God's forgiveness and tried to move forward. As his failures became more frequent, though, he became more depressed. He told me he had known for a few weeks that he should confide in me about his struggle, but there always seemed to be good reasons not to do this. He didn't want to take up my time; he needed to pray more; he was too busy to take time out for this. Finally, when he realized he was arguing with himself about this issue, he realized he needed to confess. When he told me about his struggle, I offered no profound insight or counsel. I listened, asked a few questions, and reaffirmed my belief in him. Then we prayed together. By bringing this sin into the open, God freed him from its power and hope returned to his heart. We both praised God for his provision of Christian friendship.

What is your tendency in this area? Do you have a hypersensitive conscience, overreacting to your sins? Do you wrestle with thinking that God won't forgive you unless you have confessed to someone else and done something to make up for your sins? Many of us have legalistic tendencies like this, and confessing our sins to others may be perpetuating a habit of trying to pay for our sins instead of trusting God's promise that he forgives us. When this is the case, it may be best to resist the desire to confess. Most of us, however, tend to hide our sins and struggles. We tell others about our problems only after resolving them rather than while we are struggling and failing. If this is your tendency, it is healthy to initiate openness about your moral struggles with your Christian friends on a regular basis. If you're in doubt, why not share your struggles with another Christian friend?

Take Responsibility

Biblical confession always involves taking responsibility for moral wrongdoing. Since confession means "saying the same thing" that God says, it involves agreeing with him that we sinned and admitting this to those to whom we are confessing. No admission of wrong, no confession.

"I was wrong." Why are those three words so incredibly difficult to utter? Why do excuses for remaining silent seem so persuasive? ("Now isn't the right time—I'll tell him later."). Why do mitigating circumstances seem so important? ("I was under pressure when I did it."). Why is there so much internal pressure to minimize and rationalize our sins? ("If she hadn't been so nasty to me, I wouldn't have had an affair."). The most common reason is a legalistic way of relating to others. "Legalism" in this context means basing our acceptance on our performance. If I relate legalistically to others, I believe they will accept me only if I perform up to their standard. When I fail to meet this standard (as I invariably do), I am in danger of being rejected—and rejection is one of the most painful human experiences. For this reason, there is great pressure to hide or deny wrongs, especially from the people whose acceptance we value. If you live this way long enough, you can become adept at hiding your sins from others. Ironically, however, you will also become more and more lonely and fearful of rejection.

God's antidote is amazingly simple. It is called grace. Grace means that God offers to accept us completely apart from our works for him, and solely by Christ's perfect and finished work for us. When we receive Christ, God accepts us totally and permanently in spite of our ongoing failure to meet his standard. This means that our most important relationship—the relationship we have with God—is secure. That's why, as we saw earlier in this chapter, it should be relatively easy for Christians to confess their sins to God. We can afford to be honest with God because of his grace, and honesty about our sins promotes healthy intimacy with him.

This is the same reason that it should become easier to admit our sins to others. Since God has accepted us in spite of our sins, why should we fear telling others? If they reject us, this will certainly hurt—but God still accepts us and we maintain intimacy and vitality in our relationship with him. In reality, we find that we experience God's acceptance even more deeply when we risk others' rejection through confession, regardless of how they respond. Saying "I was wrong" to others becomes a way of trusting God's grace and experiencing his acceptance more deeply.

Therefore, our confessions to others should be free from excuses and accusations. There may indeed be mitigating circumstances that made it easier for us to sin, but that is not the point. The other person may indeed have also sinned against us, but that is a separate issue that we may choose to bring up at another time. Because we are secure in God's acceptance, and because love dictates humility and honesty, we should clearly state the wrong we committed and articulate why we know it was harmful. Though it is not always necessary, asking "Will you forgive me?" is one way to communicate this humility and honesty.

Sometimes, taking responsibility involves offering to make restitution. In many situations, this is not possible. If I have lashed out in anger at my friend, I can only apologize and ask forgiveness; there is no way to repair the damage of my words. If, however, I have wrecked his car and lied about it, I should offer to pay him back in full. He may choose to release me from this obligation, but a sincere confession would include an offer to make financial restitution. Sometimes we should insist on doing so even if the other person says it is not necessary.

Before leaving this subject, a note of caution: People sometimes take responsibility for sins they did not commit. Some Christians teach that in conflict situations it is more spiritual and loving to apologize, even if you honestly don't believe you are at fault. While most of us should be wary of our tendency to rationalize, this counsel is unbiblical. It is just as wrong to take responsibility for what you did not do as it is to refuse to take responsibility for what you did do. This is because confession is based on truth, not on what is pragmatically advantageous. Instead, we should stand by what we believe is true and trust God to sustain us through the consequences. It would have been personally advantageous for Martin Luther to recant his "false teaching" that God justifies us by faith alone apart from works, but he refused to do so because he was convinced his teaching was biblical. He risked his life to stand for the truth of the gospel when it was more expedient to compromise. As a result, millions have benefited from the message of grace. Our choices to stand on the truth may not have the same world-changing consequences, but they are crucial to our faithfulness to a God who values truth.

Be Sufficiently Specific

Sometimes, we want to soothe our consciences as much as possible without really coming out into the light. So we acknowledge we've been "struggling," but become vague and evasive if our friends ask us what's going on. Maybe we send up balloons through such vague confessions, hoping others will draw us out. If we want to receive the benefits of confession, however, we must be specific about our sins. "I haven't been walking with God lately" isn't confession. "I have fallen back into a habit of using drugs" is coming out in the open.

This doesn't mean we should be morbid or lurid. An unfaithful husband should be specific about the extent of his sexual sin, but going into all the details of his adulterous encounter doesn't serve any redemptive purpose. He may be motivated by a desire to punish his wife or to atone for his own guilty conscience. I may need to admit that I have become embittered toward a friend, but I shouldn't go into all the hateful thoughts I have had about him.

Sufficient specificity sometimes also involves articulating how our sin has adversely affected the other person and (possibly) Christ's reputation. If I can't explain why it was unloving to lie to my friend, I need some additional reflection.

Think It Out Beforehand

In Jesus' famous story of the Prodigal Son (Luke 15:11-32), the repentant son realized his need to confess his sin to his father. When he got home, he said "Father, I have sinned against heaven and against you. I am no longer worthy to be called your son; make me like one of your hired men." What a beautiful expression of humility! He took full responsibility for his actions instead of blaming his father or others. He articulated his understanding that his choices violated God's character and hurt his father. He cast himself at his father's mercy and relinquished all claim to his estate.

This confession was not a spontaneous statement. It was the result of reflection and careful preparation. During the long walk home, the son carefully thought through what he needed to say. "I will set out and go back to my father and say to him: `Father, I have sinned against heaven and against you.. . .'" By the time he got home, he knew exactly what he wanted to say to his father.

Some say that heart-felt confession should be spontaneous, but the Prodigal Son would not agree. By taking the time to think through what he wanted to say to his father, he was able to do it more effectively. I have found his example to be helpful many times. I don't think very well on my feet. Especially when the issues are personal and painful, I often forget things and lose my way. By preparing beforehand, I can determine what I need to say. I sometimes catch myself making excuses for my sins, or slipping in a subtle jab at the other person. I'd rather catch that beforehand so that I don't blurt it out at the time! I may even need to make written notes to remind me if I get flustered and forget what I wanted to say. This may not be the most natural way to communicate, but being natural isn't the goal. Being honest and accurate is the goal, and preparation helps.

Discussion Questions

1. Many Christians avoid confession because they fear that others will no longer respect them. How would you respond to this line of thinking?

2. What is the connection between believing God's grace and confessing your sins to others? Why do people who avoid confession often have legalistic views of God's acceptance?

3. Share a specific example of when you confessed a sin to another Christian. What was the result? How did it affect your relationship with the other person? How did it affect your relationship with God?

7

Forgive One Another

Be kind and compassionate to one another, forgiving each other,
just as in Christ God forgave you.
Ephesians 4:32

If you love people and really get involved with them, you can count on the fact that they will disappoint, offend, betray, and hurt you! This is an inevitable consequence of relating closely to sinful people. Eventually, you will have a choice to make—withdraw from relating to people, or learn how to forgive. This is one reason why Jesus and the apostles insist that forgiveness is central to Christian love. It is an expression of love, and it enables us to go on loving. Forgiveness is one of the most powerful and liberating dimensions of the Christian life, but it can also be confusing. Let's begin our study of forgiveness by looking at its alternative.

The Alternative to Forgiveness: Bitterness

In Ephesians 4:32, Paul calls on us to "be kind and compassionate to one another, forgiving each other. . . ." This is God's alternative to bitterness (vs. 31), which is linked with ". . . rage and anger, brawling and slander, along with every form of malice." Bitterness is prolonged retributive anger toward another person because of an offense committed.

The *occasion* of bitterness is always an offense committed.[1] Many kinds of offenses may be the occasion of bitterness. Usually, the more intimate the relationship or the more heinous the offense, the more likely we will struggle with bitterness toward the offender. The list is long because people are incredibly creative in their ability to hurt one another: sexual abuse, marital infidelity, public humiliation, unfair parental discipline, relational neglect, favoritism. One may become bitter without even sustaining personal offense. We can "take up the offense" of another person who is close to us and choose to hate people who have never harmed us.[2]

"I resent George because he humiliated me. If he humiliated you, you'd hate him too!" This is the language of a determinist. George's humiliating statement made me bitter. If he humiliated you, you would have no choice but to become embittered. However, while offense is always the occasion of bitterness, it is never the cause. According to the Bible, bitterness is a chosen response to offense. This explains why two different people can experience the same offense, yet one becomes embittered while the other does not. The reason for this is not that one person was more susceptible to bitterness than the other (as though bitterness is a virus). Rather, one person chose to respond properly to the offense while the other chose to respond wrongly. This fact is painful to accept when you are bitter, but it also provides the path of liberation, as we will see.

The Half-Truth That Is a Whole Lie

What is the lie that bitter people believe? That they have the right of retribution—the right to pay people back for their offense. Deep within the human heart lies the awareness that somebody has to pay. We have a deep-seated conviction that people should pay for hurting others. This conviction is correct. It has been stamped into our hearts by a Creator who hates sin because it offends his character and destroys the creatures he loves. It is wrong, however, for us to arrogate to ourselves the right to exact retribution, because God reserves this right exclusively for himself. This is why Paul says, "Do not take revenge, my friends, but leave room for God's wrath, for it is written: 'It is mine to avenge; I will repay,' says the Lord" (Rom. 12:19). When we feel outrage over someone's sin against us, we are operating as God designed us. This is why God says there is such a thing as anger without sin (Eph. 4:26). When we choose to pay people back for their offenses, though, we are usurping God's prerogative. We are playing God—which is an even more serious offense.

What Does Bitterness Look Like?

Since bitterness is prolonged retributive anger, it always betrays itself in think-ing and behavior designed to pay the person back for his or her offense. Many people, ignorant of God's prohibition against bitterness, display this intent overtly. They shout their hatred, plot their revenge, and then boast about it to others. The revenge motif is one of the most popular plot lines in literature and cinema—precisely because most people think it is right to get even. In a way, this overt bitterness is easier to deal with because it is out in the open. If I know I hate someone, then once I know that God wants me to change my attitude, I can set about cooperating with him to forgive.

Many Christians deny they are bitter because they know God forbids bitterness. "I know God says it's wrong to be bitter—so I am not bitter." When we have hidden bitterness in our hearts, its symptoms become more subtle, but it still manifests itself if we know where to look.

We will maintain the right to pay back the offender by cultivating certain mental habits. We may replay the offense in our minds repeatedly. This memory becomes a default setting into which we move when our minds are unoccupied by other matters. We may also ruminate over the offense's negative consequences in our lives: "I spent three years getting out of debt because he fired me unjustly! It was horrible not being able to buy my children the gifts they wanted. I wore clothes until they were threadbare!" Over time, we learn to clutch and fondle such memories as perverted treasures. As a result, we will usually develop an unrealistically negative view of the offender. By focusing inordinately on his offense, we magnify his bad qualities and gradually lose the ability to recognize his good qualities. Our perception of him becomes more and more distorted so that he becomes the antithesis of all that is good and loving—the enemy who has ruined my life.

No matter how much effort we expend to hide it, we will also inevitably express this right to take vengeance. When God opens our eyes to see it, this can be extremely painful. We rejoice when the offender fails or experiences adversity. Why? Because he is getting what he deserves. Conversely, we cannot rejoice when he succeeds or experiences prosperity. Instead, we get angry because he is unfairly getting off the hook.[3] We have an inordinate desire to criticize the offender. When his name comes up in conversation, we feel a strong desire to throw in something negative. If the talk is already negative, we make it more so. If it is positive, we bring people back to reality by reminding them of his faults.

We develop a radar-like sense for finding others who are bitter toward the same person. There is a perverted but exquisite delight in commiserating with another like-minded hater over the wickedness of a common offender. I once noticed that when a friend got together with her sister, they almost immediately began to speak negatively about their stepfather. This topic would invariably dominate their conversations. They seemed to feed off of each other, even though they left such conversations drained and depressed. She was enslaved by this habit, but she was oblivious to it until I pointed it out.

Some bitter people devote much of their thought lives to fantasies of revenge. Such fantasies may simply involve giving the offender a good tongue-lashing; others are far more violent. It's easy to see why Jesus connected hatred with murder—the vast majority of homicides in the U.S. are simply the outgrowth of bitter, hateful thoughts nurtured over time. Usually, however, we take vengeance in a variety of more subtle ways. Some blow up over relatively minor issues because they give them a "reason" to spew anger that has been brewing for months or years. Others may choose to give the offender the silent treatment or engage in passive rebellion—and then deny they are angry when asked. Still others become adept at pushing the offender's buttons until they get angry, because this provides additional justification to go on hating him. Some simply sever the relationship without any explanation.

The Consequences of Bitterness

Bitter people are hurting their offenders to pay them back, but a tragic irony occurs. By taking vengeance, they hurt themselves worse than they hurt their offenders. Even worse, they injure themselves worse than their offenders injured them originally. As one astute observer put it, "Harboring bitterness is like shooting yourself to hit your offender with the recoil of the gun!" Consider the consequences of usurping God's prerogative.

The Emotional Consequences

Bitterness will poison your emotional life. There seems to be a connection between bitterness and depression. Many embittered people complain of chronic, unexplained depression. They don't seem to have the emotional resilience to circumstantial adversity they once had. God evidently designed us to have an emotional reserve that acts as a buffer to adverse circumstances. We fill this emotional reserve primarily by cultivating gratitude toward God and by practicing love toward others. Cultivating and maintaining bitterness, by contrast, takes up much emotional energy and therefore places a real drain on our emotional reserves. Consequently, bitter people often find themselves easily depressed.[4]

The Relational Consequences

When we become embittered toward another person, we usually think our bitterness will negatively affect only that relationship. We think we can tolerate this sin in our lives and yet isolate its destructive effects, but harboring bitterness will greatly impede our ability to develop and sustain any healthy relationships.

Some people seem to have a floating bitterness. Their real bitterness may, for example, be rooted in their attitude toward parents who repeatedly humiliated them. They may live a thousand miles away from their parents, yet flare up with incredible anger when anyone embarrasses them. This obviously impedes their ability to develop and sustain close friendships because embarrassment is inevitable in this context.

Long-term bitterness has a way of poisoning your personality with negativity. Embittered people tend to become cynical and full of self-pity. Over time, these destructive attitudes can even affect the way people speak and carry themselves. They develop an angry tone of voice, or a nasty facial expression, or even a hostile bodily posture. Most of us have known people whose whole bearing communicates that they are deeply angry people. Tragically, such people tend to repel others, and then become more embittered against people for rejecting them.

Most bitter people complain that their offenders have used their power to wrongly hurt or control their lives. In most cases, this is the truth. The sexual offender, the domineering parent, the abusive spouse have all used their position of authority or trust to take advantage of their victims. The tragic irony is that bitterness perpetuates and increases our offenders' control over us. The more immersed we become in rehearsing their offense and expressing our revenge, the more we allow them to dominate our lives.

This is why bitter people often become like their offenders in certain key ways. We were victimized by their abusive anger, but then we become abusive in our own anger. We were victimized by their controlling behavior, but then we become excessively controlling in our relationships with others. In a mysterious way, bitterness reduces us to the level of the people we hate. In usurping God's role to judge our offenders, we become like the very people we judge.

The Spiritual Consequences

The most precious privilege of the Christian life is enjoying relational close-ness with a forgiving God. While bitterness will not cause God to reject us, it will eventually rob us of the ability to enjoy our relationship with him. Consider John's warning in 1 John 2:9-11:

> Anyone who claims to be in the light but hates his brother is still in the darkness. Whoever loves his brother lives in the light, and there is nothing in him to make him stumble. But whoever hates his brother is in the darkness and walks around in the darkness; he does not know where he is going, because the darkness has blinded him (NIV).

Bitterness produces spiritual blindness because it is so profoundly hypocritical. Christians are the recipients of an incredible forgiveness. We are guilty before a holy God who has just cause to reject us and condemn us forever. Like the man in Jesus' parable, we expect to make others pay their debts to us while we have our own, greater debt forgiven. We insist on the right to take vengeance on our offenders, but we want to enjoy the benefits of being forgiven by God.

This double-mindedness is extreme. If we choose to retain our right to hate others, we forfeit the privilege of experiencing God's mercy and goodness. When we sever this crucial linkage between receiving God's forgiveness and extending it to others, we become spiritually paralyzed. Our Christian lives will shrivel away from what they once were when we allowed the wonder of God's mercy for us to spill out onto others.

What Is Forgiveness?

There are only two barriers to forgiveness. One is simple unwillingness, which is something each of us can decide to change. The other is misunderstanding what biblical forgiveness is. Forgiveness can be confusing, and misinterpretations of Scripture and other cultural misconceptions have distorted its meaning. As we sharpen the focus on God's view of forgiveness, note which issues have been misconceptions for you and which are issues of unwillingness.

FORGIVENESS IS NOT:	FORGIVENESS IS:
dismissing the offender's moral responsibility	dismissing the right to pay back and assuming the responsibility to love
primarily a feeling	primarily a choice based on truth
forgetting the offense	deciding not to use the offense in retributive ways
a once-for-all event	a decision which often must be reaffirmed
agreeing to trust an untrustworthy person	being willing (when appropriate) to allow the offender to rebuild responsible trust
passively tolerating future abuse	exercising disciplinary measures with redemptive intent
the same as reconciliation	being willing to work toward reconciliation

Misconception 1: Forgiveness Means Dismissing Moral Responsibility

Some people try to deal with their bitterness by resorting to a form of popular determinism. Our offenders committed hurtful acts, but they are not responsible because they themselves are the victims of other people and circumstances. If we can convince ourselves that our offenders couldn't help what they did, we may not have to face the pain of the offense and the responsibility to forgive. In a word, this is a way of playing the ostrich—keeping our heads in the sand instead of dealing with the problem.

God's Word agrees that our environment can influence us, but there is a crucial difference between influence and determinism. Christians have a basis for genuine empathy for even the most wicked criminals. Because of the Fall, all of us have an inner inclination toward evil that makes us susceptible to external temptation. In a recent television program, a reporter interviewed two of the women who killed for Charles Manson. As I listened to their explanation of how they became merciless killers by making a series of wrong choices, I realized that I could have wound up in the same horrible state. Like them, I rebelled against my parents. Like them, my rebellious attitude attracted me to immoral people. Like them, I altered my mind with drugs. Like them, I seared my conscience as I chose to do things that I knew were wrong. How would I have responded to Charles Manson if I had met him at that point in my life? As I listened to these two women express apparently genuine remorse for their crimes, my heart went out to them with compassion. I was shocked to hear the commentary of their prosecuting attorney: "These girls were different than you and me. We could never have done what they did. They were evil in their hearts in a way that you and I could never be." These words betrayed not only a lack of compassion, but also a self-righteous blindness to the wickedness of his own heart.

Empathy and compassion, however, must stop short of determinism. I can identify with these two women because I too am a sinner, but this does not remove their responsibility for what they did. At some level, their wills were operative in all of their crimes, and they came under the increasing influence of Charles Manson because they chose to turn away from what they knew was right. To decide that they were not responsible for their actions creates an endless sequence of victims (including Charles Manson). Such thinking reduces humans to mere robots, completely programmed by their environment and therefore incapable of love as well as hatred.

Biblical forgiveness always insists on personal moral responsibility, but it transfers the right of retribution to the One to whom this rightfully belongs. When I forgive an offender, I do not decide he couldn't help what he did to me. Rather, I decide that it is not my place to pay him back. God alone has this right because all sin is first of all an act of rebellion against him, and because he is the only competent moral Judge. In transferring this crime to a higher court, I am not overturning justice—I am cooperating with God's perfect justice.

Misconception 2: Forgiveness Is Primarily a Feeling

Many intense feelings may accompany forgiveness: tender compassion may replace seething rage, desire for reconciliation may replace cold alienation. Just as bitterness poisons our emotional lives, forgiveness will affect them positively. God's Spirit is able open our eyes so that we view our offenders with his mercy. He is able to cleanse our hearts so that they go out to our offenders with desire for their good. Genuine forgiveness is a miracle of God's grace that affects our emotional lives.

The Bible, however, describes forgiveness primarily as a choice based on the truth, not as a feeling. God does not say "feel mercy," he says "show mercy because I showed you mercy." I can choose against my feelings to lay down my right to exact revenge, because this is the only consistent response for a wicked sinner who has received God's forgiveness. I can likewise choose against my feelings to serve my offender in love. True, God must empower me to do this, but he promises to do this as I turn to him in prayerful trust and obedience.

Most of the positive emotional changes associated with forgiveness are the result of this choice. If I wait to forgive my offender until I feel warm toward him, I will probably wait forever. In addition, the change in my feelings toward my offender may be gradual. This doesn't necessarily mean I have not forgiven; it may mean only that my emotions haven't caught up with my choice yet. Actions are a much more reliable indicator. Am I turning away from negative thoughts that emerge in my mind? Am I refusing to follow through with the hurtful words and actions that sometimes suggest themselves? Am I choosing to pray for him and treat him with appropriate kindness?

Misconception 3: Forgiveness Is a Once-for-All Event

Have you ever decided to forgive someone, and then later realized you needed to forgive him again? Many Christians conclude from this that their original forgiveness must have been inauthentic. If they had really forgiven, they reason, their forgiveness would be like God's—complete and permanent.

Although our forgiveness should be like God's forgiveness in many ways, this is not one of them. For one thing, God knows the complete extent of our sins when he forgives us. We, however, sometimes learn more about the extent of our offenders' sins against us. A rape victim may learn that her infertility is a consequence of her offender's physical abuse. This new knowledge necessitates another decision to forgive, this time on a deeper level. Offenders may repeat their offenses in varying degrees, and we may choose to take back the forgiveness that we previously granted. The point here is that, although forgiveness is an existential choice, in many cases it looks more like an ongoing process than a crisis that is over forever. Rather than engaging in introspection about the genuineness of our original choice to forgive, we will do better if we choose to forgive again and then move forward in our walks with God.

Misconception 4: Forgiveness Is Forgetting the Offense

Many Christians say, "forgive and forget." If you have really forgiven someone, they say, you won't ever think about how he sinned against you. If you do think about it, this is the proof that you never really forgave him.

This erroneous view of forgiveness derives from a misinterpretation of Jeremiah 31:34, where God says, "For I will forgive their wickedness and will remember their sins no more." The point here is not that God literally erases our offenses from his awareness. God is omniscient—he knows (and remembers) everything. Furthermore, he disciplines Christians out of his loving concern for our good, and this discipline presupposes that he takes note of our sins. Rather, Jeremiah 31:34 means that God will never again remember our sins against us—he will never use them as a basis for condemning or rejecting us—because he has fully satisfied his righteous wrath against our sins through the death of Christ (1 John 2:2).

Biblical forgiveness means waiving the right to focus on past offenses as an excuse for hating the offender or plotting revenge. It also means choosing not to use these offenses against the person in the future through reminders, gossip, and other forms of retaliation. It may be necessary to speak about the offense at times, but the motivation for doing so will not be retribution.

What can you expect to experience concerning your memory of forgiven offenses? Because you have laid down the right to pay the person back, you will not purposefully recall and ruminate over the offense. In general, therefore, it will play a smaller and smaller role in your thought life. This doesn't mean, though, that memories of the offense will never emerge into your mind. Various events (conversations, dreams, related memories) may trigger your memory, sometimes with alarming emotional intensity. When this happens, you should not focus on the fact that you remembered the offense or experienced negative emotions along with the memory. Rather, you should focus on how you will respond to this memory. There is no reason to beat yourself for having this memory—you didn't have control over this. The best thing to do is to confront this memory with two other memories—the memory of your forgiveness by God and the memory of your choice to forgive our offender. Then choose to move forward by setting your mind on something that is true and good.

Misconception 5: Forgiveness Means Trusting an Untrustworthy Person

Many people are unwilling to forgive their offenders because they think forgiveness is synonymous with trust. If you forgive someone, this means you must trust him even though he may still be untrustworthy. Does forgiving a sexual offender mean that you entrust your young children to his care? Does forgiving a thieving church member mean that you allow him to handle collections? Does forgiving someone's dishonesty mean that you go on believing everything he says?

Forgiveness and trust, though related, are nonetheless distinct. Forgiveness relates to a past offense. It chooses to accept the painful consequences and sets the offender free from our retribution. Forgiveness, therefore, is something we choose to grant freely, with no strings attached. Trust, however, relates to the present. It is a measure of the confidence we have in a person's reliability. Trust is earned. This is precisely why we speak of people being "trustworthy"–they have proven themselves to be worthy of our trust in an area because of their reliable performance. Trusting an untrustworthy person is not spiritual; it is foolish (you may get burned), irresponsible (others may be injured), and unloving (you refuse to discipline the offender).

It is possible and common, then, to grant someone forgiveness while still insisting that he or she earn back your trust. Those who insist on being trusted just because they admitted their sins are especially suspicious, because they would probably not grant this request if they were in the other person's shoes. After confessing that I had been lying to them for years, my parents forgave me–but they didn't trust my word for a long time afterward. My initial, immature response was outrage. After all, I was genuinely sorry for my lying and I was now telling them the truth. Upon reflection, however, I realized that they could gauge my heart only by my actions, and my actions rightfully told them I was untrustworthy. Their mistrust was valid, and it taught me to place greater value on their trust.

Likewise, when people betray important responsibilities in ministry, we should forgive them freely. We would be irresponsible, however, to allow them to resume these responsibilities until they demonstrate repentance by establishing a proven record of reliability in this area.

Biblical forgiveness is different from trust, but it often involves the willingness to allow the offender to rebuild responsible trust. Forgiveness keeps its eyes open, but it desires to see restoration of this important part of the relationship.

After getting burned, we may decide never to trust offenders again in any area, no matter what they do to change. At this point, the refusal to trust has probably become retributive.

Misconception 6: Forgiveness Means Passively Tolerating Future Injury

Some Christians view forgiveness as adopting a doormat posture toward an offender. The idea of pressing charges on a physically abusive spouse, for example, seems to some people incompatible with extending forgiveness. Since forgiveness means not paying people back, doesn't this mean we should not make our offenders experience any negative consequences for their sins? Many people are quick to foster this view so they can go on preying on others, but such a view is a serious distortion of biblical forgiveness.

According to the Bible, forgiveness is an expression of love—and the love that extends forgiveness also disciplines. It is willing to confront offenders, to allow them to experience the natural consequences of their sins, and even to creatively devise consequences to influence their lives for good. Jesus chose to give himself to his captors because it was God's will for him to die for our sins, but he never allowed people to run over him because they wanted to. He "felt a love" for the rich young ruler, and because of this he exposed his idolatrous love of money (Mark 10:21). He told the Laodiceans, "Those whom I love I rebuke and discipline. So be earnest, and repent" (Rev. 3:19).

The same Paul who says, "Do not repay anyone evil for evil ... Do not take revenge, my friends, but leave room for God's wrath ... Do not be overcome by evil, but overcome evil with good" (Rom. 12:19-22) goes on to inform Christians that civil government is "God's servant, an agent of wrath to bring punishment on the wrongdoer" (Rom. 13:4). God forbids the vengeance-taking of personal bitterness, but he acknowledges that Christians may resort to the police to protect them from thieves. While some people use the civil authorities to take vengeance on their enemies, we can involve them out of love as an expression of discipline when other lesser disciplines have failed.

Misconception 7: Forgiveness Is the Same As Reconciliation

One author defines authentic forgiveness as "the mutual recognition that repentance is genuine and right relationships are achieved."[5] In this view, forgiveness is a synonym for reconciliation. Laying down the right to take retribution and reassuming the responsibility to love are the first steps toward forgiveness, but until both parties have resolved their issues, repented of their sins, and restored their relationship, forgiveness has not occurred.

While this view is commendable for its emphasis on restoring estranged relationships, it is incorrect. Reconciliation is the restoration of a relationship because both parties have resolved the enmity that separated them. It is, therefore, always bilateral. Both parties must be willing to reconcile a relationship. As many divorcees know by painful experience, one spouse who is willing to forgive and work on the marriage is not enough to ensure its success. Forgiveness, by contrast, is a unilateral decision to release an offender from my retribution. We can forgive others regardless of whether they ever repent or agree to work on their relationships with us.

Reconciliation is normally a goal of forgiveness, and forgiveness is a condition for reconciliation—but they are not the same thing. Paul makes this distinction in the way God deals with us. In 2 Corinthians 5:19, he says that through Christ's death God has extended forgiveness to all people ("not counting their sins against them")—even to those who are non-Christians. He goes on, however, to appeal to those who have not yet received this forgiveness to "be reconciled to God" (2 Corinthians 5:20). Because God has extended forgiveness, reconciliation is possible—but it does not occur unless we choose to receive his forgiveness and thereby become reunited with him. If we choose to continue our rebellion against him and deny our need for his forgiveness, we remain separate from God and justly under his judgment.

What does it mean if you claim to have forgiven someone, yet have no desire to be reconciled with him? It depends. In a fallen world, relationships sometimes break beyond repair. Physical death, for example, can permanently prevent reconciliation. By God's grace, though, we can forgive even these people and move forward in our walks as a result. If your reticence is due to his refusal to repent, your position may be justified. In this case, you may simply be saying that you refuse to act as though the issue is resolved when it is not. If, however, you are unwilling to consider reconciliation of any sort regardless of his demonstrated repentance, you may have deceived yourself about having forgiven him.

Conclusions

Has God convicted you of unresolved bitterness as you have read this chapter? If so, please respond to his conviction by telling him you are willing to forgive, no matter what this entails. As you adopt this posture before God, he will show you what specific steps you will need to take, and you will reap the benefit of a renewed vitality in your relationship with him. What good reason is there for delaying?

Discussion Questions

1. "Christians who regularly refuse to forgive others usually believe they must earn God's acceptance." Do you agree with this statement? Why or why not?

2. Share what misconceptions about forgiveness this chapter revealed.

3. Describe what it was like to refuse to forgive someone who sinned against you. What consequences did you experience? If you forgave that person, what benefits did you experience?

8

Accept One Another

Accept one another, then, just as Christ accepted you, in order to bring praise to God.
Romans 15:7

Loving one another as Jesus loves us involves accepting one another. Like any of the "one another" passages, this one is not quite as simple as it sounds.

What Kind of Acceptance?

Christians must practice more than one kind of acceptance. There is obviously a sense in which we should accept non-Christians in the same way Jesus did. They were drawn to him in a way that was strikingly different from their reaction to the religious leaders of their day. The scribes and Pharisees were generally self-righteous, uptight, and condemning toward the common people. After all, their name for them was the "sinners" (Matthew 9:10)! Not surprisingly, the people concluded that God was disgusted by them. But with Jesus, it was different. He talked openly about their sins and their spiritual lostness. They knew he was very different from them in many ways. But they sensed his genuine love for them, and he communicated God's desire to know them and his willingness to forgive them in spite of their sinfulness. They were drawn to this amazing combination of truth and love. No wonder he became known as "the friend of sinners" (Matthew 11:19)!

Unfortunately, many Christians today communicate more like the Pharisees than like Jesus. When people find out I am a Christian, I often see a noticeable change in our conversation. They get uncomfortable, they apologize for their language, they don't know how to relate to me. Why the sudden change? In most cases, it is because of their previous contact with other Christians. They are used to Christians being stiff, religious, and condemning. For this reason, one of our greatest challenges in relating to non-Christians is to overturn this misconception of a rejecting God and showing them God's willingness to accept them as they are.

This is what Paul means when he says, "Conduct yourselves with wisdom toward outsiders, making the most of the opportunity. Let your speech always be with grace, seasoned, as it were, with salt, so that you may know how you should respond to each person" (Colossians 4:5-6). Paul's emphasis here is not on the content of our speech with non-Christians, but rather on the manner of our speech. Wise Christians cultivate a conversational style that expresses God's acceptance toward non-Christians. It is this genuine attitude of love and acceptance that often inspires an interest in the message of Christ.

This is not the acceptance Paul has in mind in Romans 15:7. Here, he is referring to an acceptance Christians should express to one another. In spite of our many possible differences, we have the most important things in common. As true believers in Christ, we have a level of unity that we do not share with non-Christians because we are spiritually united to the same Lord. The same Holy Spirit dwells in us. We share a common forgiveness. We acknowledge God's Word as our common source of authority. We are also (hopefully) intent upon the same purpose—to reach out to those who don't know Christ and build up those who do know him. Because of these great commonalities, God calls on us to accept one another on a far deeper level.

This kind of acceptance is active rather than passive. The word for "accept" (*proslambano*) is a strengthened form of a word meaning "receive." *Proslambano* means to "enthusiastically welcome." Luke uses this word in Acts 28:2 to describe the kind of reception Paul received from the islanders of Malta after being shipwrecked there: "[They] showed us extraordinary kindness; for because of the rain that had set in and because of the cold, they kindled a fire and received (*proslambano*) us all." The Maltans didn't merely allow them to stay; they actively offered hospitality. Paul uses this same word to describe how Philemon should respond to the return of Onesimus, his runaway slave who has now met Christ: "if you consider me a partner, welcome (*proslambano*) him as you would welcome me" (Philemon 1:17). Their common bond in Christ should transcend their different social and legal status, and Philemon should take the initiative to make his new spiritual brother feel welcome upon his return. .

To accept one another as Christians, then, means to actively affirm our unity as members of God's family, and to relate to one another on this basis rather than on the basis of our many differences. If you have been a Christian for a while, you know this is not as simple as it may sound. Before we examine at what accepting one another looks like in practice, we need to think about a related area.

Two Equal but Opposite Dangers

As we consider how to show acceptance to those who claim to believe in Christ, things get more complicated. If we show acceptance on matters that the Bible forbids us to accept, we become guilty of *spiritual compromise*. If we fail to show acceptance to those who, while differing from us on other matters, agree on essential issues, we become guilty of *spiritual bigotry*. Navigating between these two errors is not easy, but with God's help we must do it if we are to maintain a healthy witness to a lost world.

Compromise

God has given us a body of essential truths in his Word. These truths provide the objective framework for knowing God and living for him. Think of these truths as a bold-lined circle. Some of these truths are doctrinal in content, while others are moral. Together they make up the heart of the Christian worldview. Within this circle of truth, there is freedom for us to differ in many areas, some of which are more important than others.

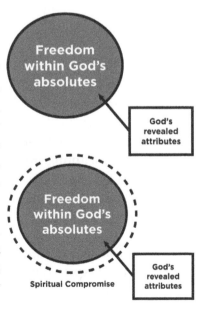

But outside of the circle is something less than true Christianity. The Christian church is a community under the truth. Certain truths are so important that there can be no unity without agreement on them. Spiritual compromise occurs when we are willing to extend this circle beyond the limits prescribed by the Bible itself.

This is why the New Testament authors make such strong statements concerning those who claim to be Christians but refuse to bow to the truth of God. For example, consider John's advice on how Christians should respond to teachers who rejected the full deity and humanity of Jesus:

> Anyone who goes too far and does not abide in the teaching of Christ, does not have God; the one who abides in the teaching, he has both the Father and the Son. If anyone comes to you and does not bring this teaching, do not receive him into your house, and do not give him a greeting; for the one who gives him a greeting participates in his evil deeds (2 John 1:9-11).

While we should show these people the same kind of acceptance we would show other non-Christians, we should not accept them as authentic Christian teachers. This distinction is crucial, because to blur it compromises biblical truth. Paul made the same distinction as he dealt with those who claimed to believe in Christ, but insisted on good works along with faith for God's acceptance (see Galatians 1:6-9; Philippians 3:1-3). Other biblical doctrines are likewise so important that we must be willing to make a distinction between those who hold them and those who deny them.[1]

The New Testament authors also call on Christians to refrain from accepting those who claim to follow Christ, but practice lifestyles that the Bible condemns.

> I wrote you in my letter not to associate with immoral people; I did not at all mean with the immoral people of this world, or with the covetous and swindlers, or with idolaters; for then you would have to go out of the world. But actually, I wrote to you not to associate with any so-called brother if he should be an immoral person, or covetous, or an idolater, or a reviler, or a drunkard, or a swindler—not even to eat with such a one. For what have I to do with judging outsiders? Do you not judge those who are within the church? But those who are outside, God judges. Remove the wicked man from among yourselves. (1 Corinthians 5:9-13)

Notice that Paul makes a distinction between the acceptance we should show all people and the special acceptance that Christians should show one another. Those who profess to follow Christ, but who insist on living a lifestyle that blatantly dishonors Christ should ultimately be expelled from involvement in Christian community until they decide to submit to Christ's way in those areas. Of course, this expulsion should be a last resort, usually after repeated attempts to persuade such people to turn around (see Matthew 18:15-17). This is a costly stand to take—and one that should be difficult for us on a personal level—but Paul calls on us to take it. Both the welfare of the person involved and the witness of the church are at stake.

Our culture is becoming increasingly (and ironically) dogmatic that there is no absolute truth or morality. While its appreciation for diversity in many areas is admirable, it has no reliable way of determining when an ideological or moral issue is aberrant. As a result, those who believe that absolute truth exists find themselves subject to increasing suspicion by many in our society. Many of us have been labeled "intolerant," "close-minded," "arrogant," or "unenlightened" when we assert (no matter how lovingly), for example, that sex outside heterosexual marriage is immoral, or that Jesus Christ is the only way to God. The age of dogmatic relativism has dawned, and it has brought with it a cold intolerance for those who refuse to assent to its all-inclusive tolerance!

This development exposes us to yet another temptation to compromise. In a culture as morally secularized as our own, many Christians are tempted to elevate biblical morality to a position of greater importance than that of biblical doctrine. The signs of this are evident, as evangelicals form alliances with other non-evangelical groups to oppose the moral decline of our society. Of course, it is fine for groups who differ over doctrine to fight for common moral concerns. Such co-belligerence has a rich legacy of social reform. But co-belligerents are not allies! During World War II, the United States, Great Britain, and Soviet Russia fought together against the fascism of Germany, Italy, and Japan. They were called the Allies who fought against the Axis powers. But they were not true allies. The United States and Great Britain were allies because they truly shared a common ideological and political heritage. But Soviet Russia, while a co-belligerent, was not a true ally because of serious ideological and political differences. The events following the war quickly revealed this, as the cold war broke out.

In the same way, evangelical Christians should be careful to make a distinction between co-belligerents and allies in their battles to defend biblical morality. Perhaps it is long overdue for evangelicals, Roman Catholics, Mormons, and other groups to join in protecting the unborn and other important moral issues. But while we may share a common ideological enemy, we also have deep doctrinal differences that prevent us from being true allies. It would be ironic indeed if, in the name of resisting moral compromise with the secular world, we committed doctrinal compromise with non-evangelical groups! Yes, we should show genuine love to people in these groups and treat them with personal respect. But unless we are willing to ask serious doctrinal questions of the people with whom we agree on moral matters, and unless we are willing to make it clear that we do not agree with them on essential doctrines, we are succumbing to a sub-biblical view of Christianity. The cure of working with them on moral issues may then become worse than the disease we were trying to defeat!

Spiritual Bigotry

It is easy for Christians to become spiritual bigots. If spiritual compromise involves extending the doctrinal or moral circle beyond biblical limits, spiritual bigotry occurs when we shrink the circle to include moral or doctrinal issues that the Bible does not consider essential. This excessively narrow view of Christianity goes beyond God's written Word. If it is important that we not make the circle of Christian acceptance larger than it should be, it is just as important that we not make it smaller than it should be.

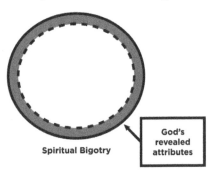

Spiritual Bigotry

God's revealed attributes

It is inevitable that Christians will have distinctives in important non-essential areas. It is also inevitable and not necessarily wrong that we will criticize each other in these areas. But when we elevate these differences to the point that we refuse to fellowship with other true Christians, or when we castigate other Christian organizations as though they were enemies of Christ, something is seriously wrong. Spiritual bigotry is just as destructive as spiritual compromise.

Spiritual bigotry, like spiritual compromise, destroys our witness to a lost world. Spiritual compromise destroys the message of truth that alone can reconcile people to God. But spiritual bigotry destroys the credibility of that message. If we want people to take us seriously when we tell them the gospel is true for everyone, we must be able to show them that people who believe the gospel can have loving unity in spite of their differences in other areas. This is not easy to do. In fact, it is impossible apart from the power and wisdom supplied by Christ. But this is precisely the miracle that God wants to do in our midst, so that "the world will know that the Father sent the Son" (John 17:23). Francis Schaeffer put it this way:

Every Christian church, every Christian school, every mission should be a community which the world may look upon as a pilot plant. When a big company is going to invest several million dollars into building a plant, it first builds a pilot plant to show it can be done. Every Christian community ought to be a pilot plant to show that we can have relationships with [each other in spite of all kinds of differences in Christ]. Unless people see [this]; unless they see that the thing that [they] rightly want but cannot achieve on a [non-Christian] base . . . is . . . practiced in our communities . . . they will not listen.. . . [2]

Spiritual bigotry also prevents us from learning and profiting from other Christians in a number of important areas. It may be comfortable to interact only with other Christians who see most things the way we do, but it is also ultimately impoverishing. We tend to develop a collective spiritual tunnel vision that gradually leads us into error or irrelevance. Interaction with other Christians has a way of correcting this tendency. Our ideas and our ways of ministering get challenged, so we have to think harder and more biblically about these things. Such thinking is crucial to spiritual health and effectiveness. Many Christians discover this principle by reading the works of Christian authors whose views differ from their own. This is a nonthreatening way to receive input and correction from the larger body of Christ. But it is often even more helpful (though also more threatening) to discuss issues face to face with other Christians who differ with us.

Practicing Acceptance with Other Christians

How do we practice this biblical mandate? We all have many areas of difference with other Christians. It is no easy task to appraise the importance of these differences and find a way to communicate biblical acceptance. The nature of the relationship and the kind of difference will affect the way we do this. Let's consider the most common differences that Christians have, and some of the ways we can communicate acceptance in spite of these differences.

Nonessential Doctrines

Because of a variety of factors, true Christians will always disagree over nonessential doctrinal matters. Some believe in predestination, while others believe in free will. Some believe in a literal millennial kingdom following Christ's return, while others believe Christ's return will immediately usher in the final judgment and eternal states. Some Christians believe that all Christians should speak in tongues at least once, while others insist that tongues is a spiritual gift that God no longer gives. Some Christians believe that women should never be elders, while others are just as adamant that female elders are normative. The list could go on and on.

Many non-essential doctrines are of relatively minor importance. Some, however, may be important enough that we would not want to get involved in a church that does not agree with us about them. For example, you may believe Christians should take communion out of a common cup, and I may believe we should use separate cups. I would hope that we could get along in the same church if this were the biggest doctrinal disagreement we had. But if you believe that all Christians must speak in tongues to show that they are filled with the Holy Spirit, and I believe speaking in tongues is a spiritual gift that most Christians do not have, we are probably going to have serious problems working together in the same church. You will probably be urging new Christians to ask God to enable them to speak in tongues, while I would view this as unnecessary and potentially harmful. Since this disagreement puts us at odds over the very definition of spirituality, we will communicate a confusing message to new Christians in our church. For this reason, it is often better for Christians who disagree on such strategically important issues to be in churches that are in basic agreement.

The fact remains that Christians who disagree with one another over important nonessential doctrines still live in the same neighborhood and work at the same company. How should we relate to one another in that setting? The first thing to realize is that nonessential doctrines, of course, are not essential. Disagreeing with another Christian over the role of tongues is a different issue from disagreeing with a Jehovah's Witness over the deity of Christ. We could not agree with our Jehovah's Witness friend to help each other bring our workmates to Christ because we don't believe in the same Christ. But we could agree to do this with a true Christian who disagrees with us about tongues. As long as we can agree on the basics of the gospel, we should agree to unite around the common goal of being lights to our common non-Christian relationships.

Some say it is best for Christians from different churches not to discuss their doctrinal differences. "Agree to disagree" is the maxim often cited. Sometimes this may be the best course of action, but this is not necessary in most cases. The problem is not discussing doctrinal differences, but rather the way we discuss them and the priority we place on discussing them. It should be possible for most sincere Christians to talk about their beliefs without waxing angry and getting into a nasty fight. As long as we agree to discuss these matters with a respectful spirit, and as long as we focus primarily and practically on how we can reach out to those who don't know Christ, such discussions can be healthy and fruitful.

We should also be able to learn from one another on matters other than the nonessential doctrines over which we disagree. If we are going to insist that the other person agree with us on every point before we're willing to learn from him, we won't learn very much! For some reason, it's easier to practice this with authors or speakers than it is with people face to face. The English writer C. S. Lewis, who died in 1963, wrote many helpful books on the defense of Christianity and on practical issues in the Christian life. I don't necessarily agree with all of Lewis's doctrinal beliefs, but I have been enormously enriched by his defense of the Christian faith. Each of us could relate similar examples. Why not search out such areas with your Christian workmates or neighbors? Such mutual learning can be deeply enriching, and it demonstrates the spirit of biblical acceptance.

Ministry Philosophy

Christian groups will also disagree on the best way to serve Christ. Some groups advocate door-to-door evangelism, while others oppose it. Some groups teach that God mandates tithing for Christians, while others hold that we should give generously and sacrificially—which will mean more than 10 percent for some and less than 10 percent for others. Some groups believe that corporate worship is the most important thing the church should do, while others believe that the first priority is local evangelism and missions. Some groups believe in congregational church government and local church autonomy, while others believe in a denominational hierarchy of leadership. Some churches stress home fellowship and every-member ministry, while other churches view these matters as optional. Again, the list could go on and on.

These issues have important and far-reaching effects on a church. They go a long way toward creating the tone or personality of a given group of Christians. For this reason, we should not minimize them. They are a reality we must deal with as we decide where to get involved and serve. Churches that are effective in ministry enjoy a large degree of agreement among their members on the ministry philosophy. It is not only that they serve a common Lord; they also agree on how to serve him. Because of this, we won't feel equally comfortable in all Christian churches. Some churches will give us a better opportunity to learn and serve than others. Some churches will be more conducive than other churches to the non-Christians to whom we are witnessing. Some churches' meetings and ministries will fit our schedule better than others.

The important thing to remember in this area is that other truly Christian groups are not the enemy. Yes, they may serve the Lord differently than we do, but they are serving the same Lord.[3] We can often find ways of working together for the cause of Christ that enable us to preserve our own distinctives while also communicating our mutual acceptance. In doing this, we can also learn from one another's strengths. We can speak well of one another whenever possible, and defend one another against invalid or unfair criticism. Such actions protect us from developing a sectarian spirit and express a practical unity that helps the cause of Christ.

Spiritual Gifts

In most Christian groups, members view certain spiritual gifts as the ones that count, while relegating others to "unimportant" status. One group may exalt tongues, another may emphasize teaching, another may highlight evangelism, while still another may promote administration. Christians with similar spiritual gifts also tend to gravitate toward one another. This can be a good thing if the main intent is to help one another to become more effective in serving others. Often, however, such groupings reinforce unbiblical ideas of superiority over the other gifts in the body of Christ. In extreme cases, as with the Corinthians, Christians are foolish enough to view their spiritual gifts as proof of their spiritual superiority.

When we use our spiritual gifts as a basis for judging other Christians' spirituality, we are acting like people who haven't met Christ. What could be more common in the world than for people to form cliques based on common talents and then use that talent as the measuring stick of acceptability? Those who are athletically gifted look down on those who aren't. The intellectually gifted view others as inferior. How foolish! Christians should realize that whatever talents we have are given to us by God, so this is no basis for superiority (1 Corinthians 4:6). Furthermore, our true value and acceptability are found in Christ through God's grace—which all Christians need and share equally.

Paul acknowledged this tendency for certain gifts to receive more honor than others—but he had a very different way of responding to it.

The eye cannot say to the hand, "I don't need you!" And the head cannot say to the feet, "I don't need you!" On the contrary, those parts of the body that seem to be weaker are indispensable, and the parts that we think are less honorable we treat with special honor. And the parts that are unpresentable are treated with special modesty, while our presentable parts need no special treatment. But God has combined the members of the body and has given greater honor to the parts that lacked it, so that there should be no division in the body, but that its parts should have equal concern for each other (1 Corinthians 12:21-25 NIV).

According to Paul, the members whose gifts receive the most honor have a special responsibility to "bestow honor" on those members whose gifts are not readily esteemed. It isn't necessarily a bad thing that you esteem teaching in your church—but the teachers should be sure to use their influence to call attention to the contribution of people who serve faithfully in other roles. One of the key features of effective and healthy churches is that their honored members consistently and sincerely cultivate this perspective. This encourages everyone to use their gifts to build up the body of Christ.

Personal and Cultural Preferences

Christians differ in the Bible translations they prefer. Some grew up with the King James Version, others with the Revised Standard, others with the New American Standard or the New International Version. Christians also differ in the musical styles they prefer. Some like the old hymns, while others like heavy metal. Christians prefer different styles of clothing. We also have different worship preferences.

The problem in this area is not the differences we have. The problem, again, is the importance we assign to these differences. If we view them as key features of our identity, we will tend to condemn those who advocate a different preference. But while God says we may freely hold and enjoy our preferences in these areas, we should be willing to subordinate them to advance the good of others. The Bible gives us two main ways to do this.

Accommodation to Non-Christians

First, we should be willing to sacrifice our personal and cultural preferences to stay culturally relevant to the non-Christians in our lives. This is Paul's point in 1 Corinthians 9:19-22,

Though I am free and belong to no man, I make myself a slave to everyone,
to win as many as possible. To the Jews I became like a Jew, to win the
Jews. To those under the law I became like one under the law (though I
myself am not under the law), so as to win those under the law. To those
not having the law I became like one not having the law (though I am
not free from God's law but am under Christ's law), so as to win those
not having the law. To the weak I became weak, to win the weak. I have
become all things to all men so that by all possible means I might save
some (NIV).

What an amazing passage! Though we are never to compromise in doctrinal
and moral areas, Paul says we should sacrificially meet non-Christians on their
cultural ground. Why? What is at stake? More people will come to Christ if we
do this than if we don't do it. People have much more trouble understanding
the message of Christ if they can't identify with the ones communicating it to
them. We may think this is unreasonable but God calls on us to demonstrate
his love for lost people in this way. After all, this is exactly what he did. God
became a human being and fully entered our world—with all the limitations and
sacrifices that this entailed—so that we could be reconciled to him. Jesus never
spoke falsehood or sinned, but he practiced the cultural identification that Paul
speaks of in this passage.

Those of us who have come to Christ out of non-Christian families know how
important this issue is. When I was twelve years old, a married couple shared
the gospel with me. From what I learned later, I am sure they were sincerely
concerned for me and accurate in their understanding of the gospel. But I
don't remember anything they said to me about Christ. All I remember was how
strangely they dressed. She may have been saying, "God loves you and wants to
have a relationship with you" but what I remember thinking is, "Why does she
wear horn-rimmed glasses?" He probably said, "Christ died for your sins so you
could have eternal life as a free gift," but I remember thinking, "Why do you
wear white socks?" There was so much cultural noise in our communication that
I never took the message seriously.

But when a friend who dressed the way I did and listened to the same music I did
shared the gospel, I heard it. This time I realized that I could become a Christian
without forsaking my own cultural identity. I suppose I should have been more
open to the adult couple, but I wasn't because cultural issues were important
to me. Thank God he sent someone with whom I could identify culturally! This

is another expression of God's grace. Just as God invites us to come to him as we are morally—without having to first change our lives—so he also invites us to come to him as we are culturally.

There has always been tension between Christians over this issue. It was part of the reason for the intense conflict over circumcision in the first century. Many Jewish Christians insisted that Gentile converts become Jews culturally (of which circumcision was the symbol) to be fully incorporated as God's chosen people. Others, especially Paul, realized God no longer required circumcision and refused to compromise because he knew this would be a significant barrier for Gentiles who heard about Christ. A bitter struggle ensued, but when the apostles realized that God no longer required cultural change in order for Gentiles to become full members of his family, they went against their own cultural preferences to cooperate with the Lord. This decision unleashed Christianity to become a truly international movement.

This theme has emerged repeatedly throughout the history of the church. Time after time, Christians have added cultural baggage to their communication of the gospel so that those outside their cultural milieu have trouble understanding the message because of all the cultural noise. Time after time, God has raised up people who have insisted on practicing Paul's mandate in 1 Corinthians 9— resulting in new breakthroughs for the gospel. Hudson Taylor insisted (against the advice of his mission society) on wearing Chinese dress and hairstyle. This was the beginning of a Chinese evangelistic movement that continues today. John Wesley insisted on preaching the gospel in the open air to coal miners who felt neither comfortable nor welcome in the church buildings of their day. The Wesleyan movement saw hundreds of thousands of working-class people come to Christ and substantially transform their society. In the late 1960s, many Christian workers met hippies on their own cultural turf—accepting their dress and hairstyles, communicating the gospel in their language, and urging them to create their own forms of worship. The result: the Jesus Movement that reached hundreds of thousands of American youths. God has consistently blessed the observance of this principle with great evangelistic fruit. When the church refuses to observe it, however, it gradually becomes a cultural anachronism that wonders why no one listens to it.

Today we are witnessing the strange reversal of this mandate in American evangelicalism. In crucial moral and ideological areas, where we should be distinct and uncompromising, evangelicals are increasingly influenced by the non-Christian culture. But in cultural areas, where we should practice conscious identification, evangelicals are becoming a distinct subculture, a Christian ghetto. Consider the amazing statistic that over half of all American evangelicals believe there is no such thing as absolute truth.[4] This represents a fundamental doctrinal compromise of the Christian message. At the same time, we see the emergence of a Christian subculture (complete with distinct musical styles, amusement parks, yellow pages) that fails to seriously identify with and engage the American culture. The result is a church that has increasing difficulty gaining a hearing for a message that is increasingly indistinct!

What does all this have to do with accepting one another? For one thing, this principle provides a limit for such acceptance. Leaders should not allow this imperative to be misused so that their church becomes culturally irrelevant to non-Christian seekers. We should personally accept one another's different musical tastes, yet insist on using music that non-Christians can relate to in open meetings. We may accept that some Christians enjoy the King James Version, but insist that those who teach use a version with more up-to-date language. We may accept that some Christians enjoy quiet and sedate social gatherings, but defend and support those who reach out to their non-Christian friends through parties with loud music. If we allow our personal preferences of Christians to set the tone for our communication to non-Christians, we are living selfish rather than sacrificial lives. Leaders should be prepared to lose members who are unwilling to sacrifice their personal cultural preferences so that lost people can more easily come to Christ.

Accommodation to "Weak" Christians

Second, we should be willing to sacrifice our personal and cultural preferences to help weaker Christians grow spiritually. This is Paul's burden in 1 Corinthians 8 and Romans 14. Some Christians believed that eating meat or drinking wine that had been sacrificed to idols would threaten their standing in Christ. They evidently also believed that they had to observe certain days as spiritually special. Paul calls these Christians "weak" in faith. In other words, their faith in Christ was not as fully instructed in these matters as it should have been. Their consciences were excessively sensitive because they had not been trained by scriptural truth to enjoy their freedom in Christ.

Other Christians knew they had liberty in such matters. Paul called these folks the "strong" in faith. Their consciences were properly informed by Scripture in these areas. Because they had been grounded in the grace of Christ, they knew no food or drink could spiritually defile them. They also knew that in Christ all days are holy, so no single day has special spiritual significance. The problem was that the "weak" Christians wanted to be like the "strong"—even to the point of imitating their behavior in these areas without understanding why it was all right for them to do so. This meant they were violating their consciences—joining in activities they erroneously thought God forbade—to gain the acceptance of the "strong." Because the "strong" prized their own freedom more than the growth of their "weaker" brethren, they were actively or passively urging them to violate their consciences. Paul called this "placing a stumbling block" before them.

Clearly, Paul's ultimate answer for this situation was for the "weak" to become "strong" in their faith. He wanted all Christians to learn about the full extent of their liberty in Christ and be freed from all superstitious restrictions.[5] In the short term, however, he urged the "strong" to limit their freedom in the presence of the "weak." If eating meat sacrificed to idols tempted a "weaker" Christian to do the same, it would be better not to eat such meat in his presence.[6] In this way, he can learn about his freedom in Christ through instruction and persuasion so that when he eats such meat, he eats it "in faith" (Romans 14:22-23).

Sadly, many Christians have misinterpreted and misapplied these passages. On more than one occasion, Christians have rebuked me for using dialogue from secular movies to illustrate a point in a Bible teaching. Some of these movies contain scenes they find objectionable. These Christians have further asked me not to attend such movies because it "stumbles" them. In almost every such case, their application of this term was inaccurate. They are not being tempted to violate their consciences and join me in seeing such movies. On the contrary, they are usually offended when I ask them if this is the case! Rather, they are saying, "It bothers me that you view them, so stop." When I offer to explain the biblical basis for my freedom in this area, they usually aren't interested. These Christians are more like the Pharisees that Jesus confronted than the "weaker" brethren of 1 Corinthians 8 and Romans 14. They knew what the Bible taught, but insisted on adding their own man-made rules to God's Word. Jesus consistently defended his freedom and rebuked them for shackling God's people with the "traditions of men." We should do the same thing with such modern Pharisees.

However, there are some situations in which "strong" Christians should be willing to limit their freedom for the sake of the "weak." Some Christians, because of past sexual abuse or immorality, simply cannot view movies with any sexual content. Because of this, it is for them a matter of conscience to abstain. Yet they may envy our freedom in this area and want to join us. In this situation, we should caution them against this course of action. And although they should cultivate the ability to be around people who drink without joining them, we should also be willing to make it as easy for them as possible. We should be able to fellowship with them over a soft drink just as easily as over a beer. After all, as Paul says, ". . . the kingdom of God is not eating and drinking, but righteousness and peace and joy in the Holy Spirit" (Romans 14:17).

Some Christians erroneously believe that they must attend a worship service on Sunday morning in order to be in God's will. Although I know differently, I should not urge them to sleep in on Sunday so they can be free. Rather, I should urge them to follow their conscience (by attending a worship meeting on Sunday mornings) while studying what the scriptures teach about this matter. I once met a Christian girl who believed that unless she ended each prayer with the phrase "in Jesus' name," God would be unhappy with her. It bothered her that I usually didn't end my prayers with this phrase. Because of her respect for me, I think I could have shamed her into doing the same thing. I could have said, "Come on! That's just a formalistic superstition. You would be more spiritual if you didn't say those words." But what would I have gained? If she followed my suggestion without understanding the biblical meaning of praying in Jesus' name, she would have only violated her conscience and possibly harmed her walk with God. I would have defended my freedom, but I would have "stumbled" her. How much better it was to tell her to keep praying in this way while we studied what the Bible teaches on this matter. Eventually, she understood why she didn't need to always use this phrase, and the problem corrected itself.

As you can see, Pharisees and "weak" Christians look similar superficially, but we should respond to them in totally different ways. We should refuse to "accept" the Pharisees' restrictions, while we should accept the "weak" Christians' limitations and be willing to limit ourselves to help them grow.

Personality Differences

God has ordained diversity in human personalities. Some people are naturally outgoing, while others are much more reserved. Some people are more intuitive, while others are more cognitive. Some people are more spontaneous, while others like to plan things out. The differences go on and on. And although each individual has a unique combination of personality traits, we can group people into basic personality types. Although our personalities can be shaped to some extent by environment, their basic orientation seems to be largely fixed from birth.

Personality differences are a key factor in close relationships. We are often attracted to people because they are different from us in personality. Take my wife and me, for example. I am slightly introverted; she is definitely an extrovert. She is fairly intuitive; I am decidedly cognitive in my approach to situations. I like to have a plan; she loves to play it by ear. Friends frequently comment on how different we are in these areas. These differences can be either a great source of pleasure and mutual enrichment, or a cause of conflict and relational pain– depending on how we handle them.

We each have personality strengths and corresponding personality weaknesses that we should simply accept and appreciate. God has created us to be different in complementary ways, and we shouldn't try to fundamentally change ourselves or each other in these areas. Although I can improve to some extent in my ability to engage strangers in conversations, I will never be as natural and effective at this as some people. How foolish it would be for me to envy them for this ability, or to condemn myself for my comparative inability. Rather, I should rejoice that I have Christian friends with this kind of personality–and thank God for the important way they communicate his love to people. I should realize I need people like this; they bring in a dimension of life I cannot supply myself.

In a similar way, I have certain temperamental strengths that many others do not have. I have always been able to see the "big picture" in issues, and I naturally tend to see the extremes to avoid. By temperament, I am a naturally "balanced" person. Since this is a personality strength, I shouldn't get frustrated because everyone else doesn't have it. God has given me this strength, in part, to help others who don't tend to look before they leap. The downside of this personality trait is that I can be indecisive. I see both sides of issues so naturally that I can be very reluctant to adopt a course of action when something must be done. It really doesn't help me when temperamentally decisive people upbraid me for my indecisiveness! Try as I might, I will never be as decisive as they are. But I appreciate it when they accept my personality, with its strengths and weaknesses, and then help me to see why a certain course of action is the right one.

We enrich our relationships immeasurably when we accept one another's person- alities in this way. We stop expending energy trying to mold ourselves or each other in ways God never meant to mold us. We become both more confident that we have something significant to contribute to our friends' lives, and more appreciative for what they contribute to us.

Personality-Related Character Weaknesses

This is not to say, however, that we should be totally passive about effecting change in one another's lives. We have already seen from previous chapters that, especially through encouragement and admonition, God wants to work through us to transform others' characters. This is true even in the character issues connected to our personalities. There are areas connected to our personalities that have a moral dimension. As fallen people, we have character weaknesses that tend to run along personality lines.

For example, along with my temperamental strength of balance and weakness of indecisiveness comes a deep-seated and self-protective fear of conflict. Especially when it involves people who have the power to hurt me, I have an ingrained tendency to avoid confronting them—even when this is clearly the right thing to do. I catch myself rationalizing on an almost subconscious level how I can avoid upsetting the relationship in this way. Even when I resolve to do this, I often wind up wimping out to some degree, compromising or not pressing the issue as far as I should. Those who know me best sometimes express dismay at this weakness, and it makes me sick to admit it to myself. I have seen God change me in this area over the years, but I can hardly boast that I have been fully transformed. It remains an embarrassing blemish in my character.

One of my best friends is a born leader. He has excellent discernment, he sees the direction we need to take, he is able to impart this vision and motivate people in this direction, and (so important for leaders) he is thick-skinned when it comes to criticism. Not surprisingly, he is not the warmest person in the world! He often doesn't notice people who say hello to him, probably because he's thinking about where God wants to lead our church! He struggles with impatience when people respond slowly to his leadership. He finds it more difficult than many to apologize or express his appreciation. I know my friend is open to God in these areas, because I have seen him change over the years. But change is slow, and in the meantime people continue to be bruised in various ways by this gifted leader. Others, especially those who don't have these character weaknesses, sometimes say "Why doesn't he just change?"

How should we view these weaknesses? Though they are definitely related to personality, they are not simply personality weaknesses. They are really moral issues. Christ's character includes things like the courage to confront, sensitivity and compassion, the humility to apologize. How do we "accept one another" in this area of personality-related character issues?

The biblical answer to this question is yet another "one another" imperative—forbearance. Addressing the importance of unity between Christians, Paul urges us to

> ... walk in a manner worthy of the calling with which you have been called, with all humility and gentleness, with patience, *showing forbearance to one another in love*, being diligent to preserve the unity of the Spirit in the bond of peace. (Ephesians 4:1-3)

In a parallel passage he says,

> ... as those who have been chosen of God, holy and beloved, put on a heart of compassion, kindness, humility, gentleness and patience; *bearing with one another*, and forgiving each other, whoever has a complaint against anyone; just as the Lord forgave you, so also should you. And beyond all these things put on love, which is the perfect bond of unity. (Colossians 3:12-14)

Forbearance is the "grease" that lubricates close Christian relationships.

In both of these passages, Paul links forbearance with patience. Forbearance doesn't mean denying others' sins or refusing to confront their character problems. This is a convenient abdication of love's responsibility. It means, rather, that we show patience as we deal with one another's sin-problems. As the word suggests, it involves the willingness to "bear with" people's moral rough edges. Out of love, we accept the fact of their deep-seated fallenness, and agree to put up with the discomfort involved in relating to this fallen person. We understand that true change will probably come slowly, and that in the meantime we will receive some of the bumps and bruises that come with relating to this person. Yes, there is a place for serious discipline and confrontation. Yes, there is a time to withdraw from closeness in a relationship because of the other person's unwillingness to change seriously damaging behavior. But not even the best relationships between growing Christians can survive without liberal doses of forbearance. Without it, we will either distance ourselves from each other and quit helping each other change, or we will get fed up with each other and end the relationship.

How can we lay hold of this kind of patience? Obviously, it begins by realizing that we are just as fallen as the people we struggle to bear with! Though our character problems usually seem less glaring than others, they are also irritating, they also cause bruises to the ones who love us. Just ask your closest friends if you don't believe this—but be ready to hear the truth! This realization can be very helpful when we are feeling fed up with others' moral rough edges.

On an infinitely more serious level, think how our character deficiencies must irritate a holy God who has no character problems at all! Yet he shows forbearance to us, he is patient with us, and he puts up with an amazing amount of imperfection in us. It is God's grace toward us, more than anything else, that motivates us to show forbearance to one another.

Conclusion

Accepting one another displays the greatness of God's character. This is what Paul means when he says ". . . accept one another, just as Christ also accepted us *to the glory of God*" (Romans 15:7). Christ's willingness to become a human and go to the cross demonstrated God's love and holiness and wisdom in a way that will never be surpassed. Through Christ, God found a way to accept sinful, rebellious people without compromising his own righteous character. Throughout all eternity, unfallen angels and redeemed human beings will continue to marvel at this incredible revelation of God's excellence.

We can do nothing to surpass this revelation, but we can do something to complement it. We can accept one another in the ways we have studied in this chapter. Although this acceptance will always be imperfect, it nonetheless displays something that glorifies God. As we learn how to relate to one another in ways that rejoice in legitimate diversity without compromising God's truth, we demonstrate something of God's character to a broken humanity that longs for unity amid diversity but does not know how to accomplish this. As we discover that our unity in Christ enables us to form love relationships with people whom we would otherwise have never befriended, we can thank God for this personal blessing that also bears witness to his greatness!

Discussion Questions

1. Discuss other examples of spiritual compromise and spiritual bigotry with which you are personally familiar. How did they damage Christ's reputation?

2. Discuss ways in which your church might collaborate with other churches that differ in non-essential doctrines and ministry philosophies, in order to practically demonstrate unity in Christ.

3. What factors would you consider in deciding whether to practice forbearance or confrontation with another person's sin?

9

Building Up the Body of Christ

. . .speaking the truth in love, we will in all things grow up into him who is . . . Christ. From him the whole body, joined and held together by every supporting ligament, grows and builds itself up in love. . .
Ephesians 4:15-16

Being a human being is complicated business. We have so many desires, many of which seem to be in conflict with one another. Some of these desires are truly contradictory—we need to choose for some and against others. For example, I sometimes desire to become materially wealthy. There are many seemingly good reasons for following this desire, but the Bible warns me not to do this because it is idolatry (Matthew 6:24), which will also ultimately result in personal misery (1 Timothy 6:9-10). Because I believe the Bible is true, I try to resist this desire and replace it with another desire that the Bible affirms—to become spiritually wealthy through sacrificial service for Christ. So I lurch along, trying to discern between these two desires, resisting one and feeding the other.

Sometimes, however, desires that appear contradictory are actually complementary. Such is the case with the subject of this chapter.

On the one hand, we all have the desire to be anonymous parts of a movement whose goals are greater than we are. On the other hand, we all have the desire to stand out as individuals, to excel in ways that show we really matter. We experience these two different desires all the time. I enjoy being one of thousands of fans rooting for my favorite basketball team. There is something uniquely exhilarating about being in an arena with thousands of other people who pull for the same team. My individual participation is almost totally anonymous, yet I derive great personal satisfaction from cheering the team on. On the other hand, I also enjoy playing basketball myself. Although I am not a star, I derive an incredible sense of satisfaction from making a good pass, blocking a shot, or sinking the winning basket. How do I reconcile these two desires? Clearly, they don't need reconciling because they are not contradictory. They are in tension to one another in the sense that they are different desires—but this tension is healthy. Being a fan and being a player go together.

Good coaches are adept at cultivating this tension in all of their players. They motivate every player to be most concerned with the overall team goals, but they also help each player to play a suitable specific role that will help the team to win. Successful coaches are quick to rebuke a player for a selfish playing style, but they will also confront players who lose sight of the importance of their individual roles. On teams with winning "chemistry," players not only have complementary skills and roles—they also have a mentality that affirms both of these desires.

This dynamic tension is present in many aspects of human society. At the workplace, everyone needs to "own" the goals of the company—and find an individual role that significantly contributes toward those goals. In warfare, an entire country must commit itself to the war effort, and every individual must contribute in a variety of ways.

What has all this to do with Christians loving one another? Lots! God instills this dynamic, creative tension in us, and it finds its ultimate fulfillment in a relationship with Jesus Christ and faithful participation in his Body, the church. Consider the following passage from this perspective:

> But to each one of us grace was given according to the measure of Christ's gift. . . . And He gave some as apostles, and some as prophets, and some as evangelists, and some as pastors and teachers, for the equipping of the saints for the work of service, to the building up of the body of Christ; until we all attain to the unity of the faith, and of the knowledge of the Son of God, to a mature man, to the measure of the

stature which belongs to the fullness of Christ . . . speaking the truth in love, we are to grow up in all aspects into Him, who is the head, even Christ, from whom the whole body, being fitted and held together by that which every joint supplies, according to the proper working of each individual part, causes the growth of the body for the building up of itself in love. (Ephesians 4:7-16)

On the one hand, every Christian is part of a team that has certain divinely set corporate goals. Through the church, God wants to bring more and more people to Christ, and he wants to bring all of those people to spiritual maturity in Christ. These are truly worthy goals for our lives, and as Christians we need to own these goals strongly enough that we sincerely rejoice when we see progress in this direction, and that we are willing to sacrifice other personal goals when they threaten to seduce us from this larger purpose. On the other hand, every Christian also has been uniquely gifted to make a significant individual contribution toward these overall goals. Each of our roles are significant because the corporate goals are affected by whether or not we choose to play our roles, and by how well we play them.

Assessing Your Involvement

Once we understand this healthy tension, we have a practical way by which we can evaluate our involvement with other Christians. Every Christian should find practical ways to express both appreciation of and participation in larger corporate goals, and find practical ways to contribute as a significant individual. Both are necessary in building up the body of Christ.

The following chart is a convenient way to think about your own involvement in God's church.

High corporate participation & low individual participation	High corporate participation & high individual participation
Low corporate participation & low individual participation	High individual participation & low corporate participation

(vertical axis: Corporate Involvement; horizontal axis: Individual Involvement)

The goal of this chart is not to fix anyone in a category, because we all can change. But it is difficult to do this unless we know where we are and which direction we need to go. Obviously, the goal is to move toward the upper right-hand quadrant—this represents God's will for our lives as expressed by Paul in Ephesians 4. Which quadrant best describes your own involvement in the church? Once you identify this, you can take practical steps to move closer toward the goal.

Low Corporate and Low Individual Involvement: Nominalism

This quadrant describes many people in the American church scene. The majority of Americans either belong to or attend a church, but their involvement is sporadic and superficial. Many Americans accept this as normal and appropriate. Indeed, this is where many of us begin in our dealings with Christ, but it is unhealthy to stay here. To do so is to settle for nominal involvement in the body of Christ.

For some, the first step beyond nominalism is the realization that coming to Christ is distinct from membership or involvement in a local church. As one evangelist regularly reminded his listeners, "Going to a church doesn't make you a Christian any more than going into a garage makes you a car!" First we need to personally receive Christ and begin a relationship with him. Then on that basis, we should become involved in a local church to grow in our relationship with Christ. The order is crucial. Healthy local churches are aware of this misconception and regularly correct it to those who attend.[1]

But the sad fact is that many true Christians stay at this low level of involvement with other Christians. The myth that "I don't need other Christians because I have Christ" is widespread in a culture like our own that glorifies individualism at the expense of community. It is therefore easy for American Christians to settle into this rut. As I have argued elsewhere in this book, however, we must be willing to become more involved with other Christians if we expect to grow spiritually and become fruitful in our Christian lives. Healthy local churches call on all true Christians to do this, and facilitate deeper involvement in a variety of ways (some of which are discussed below).

High Corporate and Low Individual Involvement: Large Meeting Anonymity

Most new Christians regularly attend large worship services or Bible studies. They have a natural hunger to learn the Bible and to be around other Christians. They consider themselves committed to their churches, and they usually are aware of and support the overall goals of the church. They may also invite their non-Christian friends to these meetings, because they want them to discover what they have received in Christ.

Many local churches regard this level of involvement as sufficient, but it falls short of the biblical standard. In fact, unless you go beyond this, your involvement will probably become boring and perfunctory before long. Once the stimulation of learning new biblical truths wears off, you may be tempted to move backward to a lower corporate involvement. Many Christians spend their Christian lives fluctuating between these two quadrants, tragically missing the excitement and fulfillment they could have with deeper involvement in the body of Christ.

Home Groups

The challenge, of course, is to begin to practice Jesus' injunction to "love one another." For most of us, this is a distinct decision to get more deeply involved with a specific smaller group of Christians. This is undoubtedly why the early church met regularly in homes as well as in large groups (Acts 2:46; 20:20; Rom. 16:4). These meetings should be more than another Bible study in a smaller meeting place. They should also provide a practical framework for the kind of ongoing relational involvement described in the New Testament letters. Ideally, new Christians should get involved in home groups as soon as (or even before) they come to Christ. In this environment, they can receive the personal care and instruction that helps them start right and grow straight.

Wise church leaders will emphasize home groups, because such groups practically facilitate greater individual involvement far more than preaching numerous sermons on the subject. No amount of biblical teaching can explain the difference between attending church and being in fellowship—because a picture is worth a thousand words. There are several keys to a healthy home-group ministry, including effective leadership training and the willingness to give lay leaders significant freedom in their ministries.[2] Today, many reading materials and conferences provide help for pastors who want to move their churches in this direction. But pastors should also get involved in home groups if they expect them to be part of the ethos of their church. Furthermore, they will not know how to train other lay home-group leaders unless they lead home groups themselves.

Personal Discipleship

Especially in the context of a home group, it is also advisable to look for opportunities to disciple younger Christians. "Discipleship" in this sense means choosing to get personally and consistently involved with a younger Christian to help him learn how to walk with Christ and serve others. It is primarily practicing the "one another" imperatives described in this book with a younger Christian who wants to mature spiritually. All Christians can eventually become effective in discipling others, and this ministry is essential for healthy church life. It is also one of the most rewarding ministries in which we can be involved. Many of us have experienced the thrill of leading another person to Christ—it's difficult to imagine anything more satisfying than this! But the apostle John, who led many people to Christ, says he found something even more fulfilling: "I have no greater joy than to hear that my children are walking in the truth" (3 John 1:4 NIV). His "children" probably were the people he had personally pastored and discipled. Nothing surpassed the joy he experienced as he saw them mature into faithful servants of Christ. What Christian parent would not be overjoyed to see his children grow into mature and responsible adults who love Jesus Christ and serve him faithfully? Those who disciple younger Christians can multiply this joy many times over.

It is relatively easy to get started in a discipleship ministry. All you need is a younger Christian who wants to grow spiritually and the willingness on your part to teach him or her what you have learned in this area. You will encounter many surprises, challenges, and some disappointments along the way, but those who get involved in this ministry usually stay with it because it is so deeply fulfilling. Experienced disciplers have recorded their insights on this subject in a number of helpful books.[3] Others in your church may have valuable experience in discipleship that they would be glad to share with you. Ideally, all the leaders and workers in your church are committed to discipling younger Christians. This creates an environment rich in insight and support. Why not take up this challenge and ask God to guide you to a hungry younger Christian you can disciple?

Ministry Utilizing Spiritual Gifts

You also need to discover and exercise your spiritual gifts in specific ministries within your church. Spiritual gifts are God-given abilities to serve others so that the body of Christ is built up. God gifts every Christian, and because God loves variety there are limitless combinations and degrees of gifting among individual Christians. Through faithfully exercising our spiritual gifts, we can make a unique contribution to the work of Jesus Christ and experience the unique satisfaction of ministering in our gifted areas.

The New Testament contains no direct instruction on how to discover one's spiritual gifts. This issue, which is the subject of so many popular books and teachings, was evidently never a pressing problem in the early church. Paul and others seem to assume that Christians can discover their gifts. They emphasize instead the importance of faithfully using these gifts to serve others in love (see Rom. 12:3-8; I Corinthians 12:4¬13:13; Eph. 4:11-16; 1 Peter 4:10-11).

Most of the scriptural passages concerning spiritual gifts occur in the context of "one another" imperatives. This fact provides us with an obvious but often overlooked clue to discovering our own gifts: Since gifts are for service, we must commit ourselves to serving others if we want to discover and develop our gifts! If we develop a lifestyle oriented around loving other Christians, our special spiritual gifts will gradually emerge. Because home groups and personal discipleship facilitate this lifestyle, these commitments also become practical steps to discovering gifts. If, by contrast, we are unwilling to consistently relate to others in sacrificial love, we will probably remain in the dark about our spiritual gifts.

Many churches provide help in assessing and deploying its members into ministries suited to their gifting, spiritual maturity, ministry burdens, and life situations. A variety of helpful written material on this subject is now available.[4] But as long as you are willing to serve God, sincerely ask for his guidance, and take some initiative, he will guide you into the ministry roles he has designed for you. God sometimes does this by drawing your attention to other Christians whose ministry in some way approximates his design for your own. Sometimes he alerts you to ministry needs that are going unmet and couples this with a desire to serve in this area. Sometimes he challenges you to serve in an area in which you feel unqualified and uninterested—and then surprises you by showing you that you are skilled in this area and enjoy it. All Christian servants have their unique stories of how God led them into their specific ministry roles. This is not surprising, since we are persons and God guides us personally. The important thing is that we follow his leadership, and then become faithful stewards of his gifts.

High Individual and Low Corporate Involvement: Silo-Culture

The business world sometimes calls this condition "silo culture." Departments can become so focused on meeting their own production quotas that they define success solely with these goals. The company may be slowly going out of business, but they feel great about reaching their goals. Or, conversely, the company may be progressing nicely, but they feel frustrated and resentful because they did not receive the allocations they wanted to accomplish the goals they set. Each department becomes a silo—separated from the other departments.

Christian workers often develop this condition. They may have close relationships and specific ministry roles, but they can easily become spiritually myopic. Immersed in their relationships and ministries, they lose sight of the big picture. They no longer see their roles as part of the greater team of which they are a part. Instead, they begin to see their roles as the most important thing—and the rest of the church as a supporting cast or competitor. They can even become resentful if they must sacrifice their individual goals so the church as a whole can move ahead.

We have had to come to grips with this mentality in our church. Fortunately, we have always emphasized the importance of individual ministry goals. We encourage home groups and ministry teams to actively plan and pursue their own biblical goals. Our church leadership has focused mainly on equipping people for ministry and delegating leadership authority to people whom God has raised up. This has resulted in an active and highly motivated work force. All of this is good, and I hope we always maintain this ethos.

But it also has its potential downside. In this environment, it is easy for some of the home groups and ministry teams—and the individuals leading those groups—to forget that they are part of a larger overall effort. They can lose sight of (and interest in) the church's corporate efforts and goals. They can even begin to view each other as competitors for the church's limited resources. When the leaders of the whole church make difficult strategic, budgetary, and structural decisions, workers sometimes communicate exasperation that their ministries didn't receive as much recognition as they would have preferred. In the worst-case scenario, ugly turf wars could develop, with whole ministries deciding to break off and go their own way because the church is holding them back.

How can we prevent this? To a certain extent, such dangers cannot be eliminated without also eliminating the motivation that comes from personal involvement in Christian fellowship and ministry. Pastors have long realized the potential for division that comes with emphasizing lay ministry and leadership. That is one reason so many pastors are unwilling to equip and deploy lay leaders extensively. Ultimately, we must decide that the benefits of this ethos are worth the risks that come with it. Besides, divisions are common even in churches that don't emphasize this level of individual ownership. Christians can always find things to fight about! Still, we can minimize the risks by taking certain steps. First, it is important for the church to meet together in large meetings. Howard Snyder explains the genius of the New Testament church's large and small group meetings in this way:

> The individual believer must be able to feel himself a pan of the larger corporate unity of the people of God. . . . The church must meet regularly as a large congregation. . . . This is one reason why small-group fellowships, essential as they are, are not in themselves sufficient to sustain the life of the church. The individual cells of the body of Christ must see and feel their unity with the larger body.[5]

In our own church, we do not have adequate facilities to meet regularly as one group. But we strongly encourage everyone to regularly attend one of our weekly large meetings, and we require home-group and ministry-team leaders to model this practical expression of involvement in the larger church. In these meetings, we come together to study God's Word and be informed about what God is doing in other parts of our church. We have an annual retreat for the whole church. This is a weekend celebration, when everyone can meet and experience the sense of being one big family. It also gives the leadership the opportunity to address everyone about the larger vision and goals of the church. We also have quarterly meetings and an annual retreat for our lay leaders, which help them maintain a healthy concern for the whole church.

Second, we can cultivate an ethic of interest in what God is doing in other parts of our church. Stay in touch with Christian friends who fellowship and minister in different home groups. Learn about what God is doing in other ministry teams, and what the overall needs of your church are. The leadership of your church should model this kind of interest and regularly communicate this information, but you can also ask and investigate. In my own home group, which is primarily for college students and career singles, we invite a different ministry team to address our group at each quarter break. Our members learn about what God is doing elsewhere in our church from people who are personally involved, and they also learn how they can get involved in those ministries if they desire to.

Third, we can commit ourselves to regularly pray for and give financially to the overall work of the church. When we take the time to pray for people and situations beyond our immediate circle of concern, we are cultivating the team spirit the Bible advocates. God increases our concern for their success, and we realize that we can be vital co-laborers through consistent intercession. Consistent and sacrificial financial giving is a way of expressing and increasing our involvement in the corporate work of the church. Over the years, I have often observed a correlation between Christian workers who develop a "silo culture" and a poor giving habit to the overall church. One might argue that the poor giving habit is the result of this mentality rather than the cause of it. This is no doubt the case in some instances, but it is equally common for financial giving to express our commitment, as Jesus noted when he said "Where your treasure is, there will your heart be also" (Luke 12:34). At any rate, cultivating this practice and advocating it to others helps us to maintain an interest in the whole church.

The New Testament calls us to have a practical concern not only for the whole local church to which we belong, but also to Christ's work throughout his whole church world-wide. Paul modeled this attitude as an apostle, and he called on Christians to pray for and help in ministries far away from their local churches. Today, through the increase in communications technology, we can do this in ways that Paul never envisioned. In fact, the amount of information can be overwhelming. For this reason, it is usually best to select a few areas of Christ's global work and be faithful in prayer and financial support. As our ability to serve increases, we can then expand our outreach in this area.[6]

Conclusion

Of the four quadrants listed above, which one best describes your involvement with other Christians? Since God wants all of us to move toward high individual and corporate involvement, he will certainly supply us with the resources to attain it. Ask God to show you what practical steps you need to take toward this goal—and then step out in faith to follow what he shows you! This path will involve some scary steps along the way, but it leads to spiritual life that is increasingly fruitful and fulfilling!

Discussion Questions

1. Which of the four quadrants best describes your participation in Christian fellowship? What factors account for this?

2. What specific steps can you take to move toward more healthy involvement in Christian fellowship?

3. Discuss how you might help other Christian friends to move toward more healthy involvement in Christian fellowship.

APPENDIX 1

Confidentiality in the Body of Christ

Is it proper to talk about our Christian friends' sins to other Christian friends, even when they don't want us to do this? How should we respond to this request: "I want to confess something to you, but you must first promise that you won't tell anyone else"? When is it right to keep such information in confidence, and when is it wrong to do so?

It is not possible to become involved in real Christian fellowship without regularly facing this issue. Because we have a network of relationships, and because we have concern for a number of people, we not only talk to each other about our own problems—we also talk with one another about our mutual friends' problems.[1]

Imagine a family in which the members talk to one another about their problems, but never talk about one another's problems with other family members. If the family is having dinner and one member is missing, what could be more natural than to ask where he is? And if he is involved something that is wrong and hurtful, what could be more natural than for the other family members to discuss this issue? What would you call a family that never engaged in this kind of discussion? "Close" and "tight-knit" certainly wouldn't be accurate.

If Christians are brothers and sisters in the family of God, should they also talk to each other about fellow family members—including talking about their sins and problems? Is this a sign of healthy Christian fellowship, or is it dysfunctional? It depends on a number of factors.

What Is the Biblical Position?

At first glance, the Bible seems to supply contradictory guidance on this issue. Numerous biblical passages urge us to be quiet about one another's sins. Numerous other passages urge us to speak up.

Don't Tell

A number of passages strongly condemn telling other people about someone's problems. The book of Proverbs is full of such warnings. "A gossip betrays a confidence; so avoid a man who talks too much" (Proverbs 20:19). "A gossip betrays a confidence, but a trustworthy man keeps a secret" (Proverbs 11:13). "He who covers over an offense promotes love, but whoever repeats the matter separates close friends" (Proverbs 17:9). "If you argue your case with a neighbor, do not betray another man's confidence, or he who hears it may shame you and you will never lose your bad reputation" (Proverbs 25:9-10). "A perverse man stirs up dissension, and a gossip separates close friends" (Proverbs 16:28).

Paul distinguishes gossip from slander. Slander is communicating information we know is false, while gossip is inappropriately communicating information we believe to be true. He tells us that both slander and gossip are manifestations of human depravity and are entirely unfitting for Christians (see Romans 1:29; 2 Corinthians 12:20). He also condemns busybodies for "saying things they ought not to" (1 Timothy 5:13; 2 Thessalonians 3:11).

Jesus tells us in Matthew 18:15, "If your brother sins, go and reprove him in private." Jesus' insistence on private confrontation implies the desirability of resolving the matter privately if possible.

We have all seen the wreckage that gossip can cause: hurt feelings, eroded trust, broken relationships. When Christians habitually engage in gossip, they create an atmosphere of mistrust that destroys community. People refuse to open up with anyone about their problems because they realize others will probably use this information against them. This is a reason why, in many churches, people live in isolation from one another. They have learned the hard way not to trust each other.

Tell

The Bible argues just as strongly for the need to tell others about someone else's sins. Because this emphasis is less familiar, I will develop it in greater detail.

Many forms of church discipline require sharing of such information. In the same passage where Jesus tells us to confront one another in private, he goes on to say that if the matter remains unresolved, we should "take one or two others along, so that every matter may be established by the testimony of one or two witnesses" (Matthew 18:16). This may refer to bringing in others who also witnessed the offense, because the one being confronted denies that he or she has committed an offense. But it can also mean that we involve others who agree that such behavior is wrong, because the one being confronted admits to the action but denies its immorality. In the latter case, of course, the new parties must be informed about the offense. Regardless of how one understands verse 16, Jesus clearly teaches in verse 17 that in some cases, we should disclose unrepentant sin to the entire church. "And if he refuses to listen to them, tell it to the church." As Christians, we have the freedom to sin—but we do not have the right to insist that other Christians hide our sins from those who need to know.

Similarly, Paul tells us that we should "not entertain an accusation against an elder unless it is brought by two or three witnesses" (1 Timothy 5:19). We should expect elders to be maligned occasionally because of the nature of their work, and we should trust their integrity enough to require solid proof that they have acted immorally. But with this protection comes a greater measure of accountability. "Those [elders] who continue in sin are to be rebuked publicly, so that the others may take warning" (v. 20). Christian leaders are public figures, and when they compromise their leadership by serious or repeated sin, they must be prepared to have this information known by others. This is probably part of what James means when he tells teachers that they will "incur stricter judgment" (James 3:1).

In Galatians 6:1, Paul says, "If someone is caught in a sin, you who are spiritual should restore him gently." The word caught probably means just that—surprised by other Christians who observe his sin. "You who are spiritual" may refer to all Christians, in which case Paul is simply repeating Jesus' command in Matthew 18:15.

But it is probable that "you who are spiritual" refers to those more mature Galatian Christians who habitually "walk by the Spirit" (Galatians 5:16,25), and who therefore can do a better job of restoring errant Christians. In this case, of course, the one who "caught" the person would need to inform the "spiritual" ones. In other words, it would be right to tell them about this person's private sins, so we can restore the offender as quickly and as effectively as possible.

Many New Testament passages speak of plural leadership in the local church. In one of these passages, 1 Peter 5:2, Peter says, "Shepherd the flock of God among you." That is, the elders of the local church should work together in supplying direction and protection and correction to the other members. This collegiate approach to shepherding, of course, implies that the elders will sometimes need to share information about members' sins to decide together how to best restore them. This is probably one reason why deacons must be "not double-tongued" (1 Tim. 3:8). Church leaders must demonstrate the ability to handle sensitive information with wisdom and discretion, precisely because they are privy to such information.

First-century Christians sometimes shared information about other Christians' sins in other ways that the apostles deemed to be appropriate. For example, in 1 Corinthians 1:11, Paul cites "Chloe's people" as his source that the Corinthian church was riddled with factions and divisions. In all likelihood, "Chloe's people" were Christians who worked for a prominent Christian businesswoman (Chloe). They may have visited Corinth on business and witnessed the problems in the church. We don't know if they confronted the Corinthians about their sins; we know only that they notified Paul of them. At any rate, it is clear that Paul regards this disclosure of the Corinthians' sins as helpful. I doubt that he would have been sympathetic to a complaint by the Corinthians that Chloe's people had no right to tell Paul about this!

The metaphor of the church as the body of Christ also argues for sharing information about one another's sins. When one member of my body has an infection, this information is somehow communicated to many other members. My liver manufactures white blood cells and sends them to the infection site. If I sprain my ankle, the rest of my muscles need to know about this so they may compensate. The members of our bodies freely share information with each other so that our bodies may grow and stay healthy. Leprosy is an insidious disease precisely because it stops the flow of information to other body members. Lepers lose fingers and toes because injuries occur and go untreated since the nerves no longer communicate pain to the rest of the body.

Since the church is the body of Christ, its members must share information with each other, not only about our own sins, but also about others' sins—so that we can help each other. As members of the same body we are affected by each other: "If one part suffers, every part suffers with it" (1 Corinthians 12:26 NIV). Therefore, we should help each other, and to do this, we must be able to know about each other's failures as well as each other's victories.

Christians are usually quick to share about their victories and eager to have that information communicated to others. But we are usually reluctant to share our defeats with others, and feel outraged if they share this information with others— even when they do this to help. If we submit ourselves to a gag rule on sharing this information, our relationships will be correspondingly superficial and our vitality and effectiveness will decrease.

If a church riddled by gossip is ugly, so is a church tyrannized by the right of individual privacy. Furthermore, such a church has conformed to the values of our secular culture. Western culture, which prizes autonomous individualism, emphasizes this right at the expense of the individual's responsibility to the community. The mentality that says "My life is my business alone and only those I wish to tell have a right to know" is one that destroys fellowship just as effectively as the mentality that shares personal information indiscriminately.

Today, it is increasingly common for Christians to share personal information only with professional pastors or counselors, and under a strictly enforced confidentiality rule. While there are situations in which such an arrangement is valid, it should not be the norm. The notion that we should share our serious problems only with professionals is not a biblical provision for Christian fellowship; it is a sad caricature of it. If we refuse to entrust information about our problems with our Christian friends, we will have increased privacy at the expense of community.

Conferral Versus Gossip

These two sets of biblical material are not contradictory. In authentic love relationships, there are times when it is best to keep such information to yourself, and there are times when it is best to share it with someone else. More specifically, there are times when such sharing is illegitimate gossip, and there are times when such sharing is legitimate conferral. Medical doctors frequently confer with one another concerning their patients' conditions. This is a standard and important feature of medical practice. Doctors can be more effective with their patients if they can draw upon one another's experience and expertise. The same kind of conferral can and should go on between Christians as they consider how to help their mutual Christian friends. Conferral is different from gossip in several important ways. Consider the following distinctions between these two forms of sharing.

- Conferral is motivated by a desire to help the other person and to build up the church. In other words, it is motivated by love. Gossip lacks this commitment to the other person's good. It is selfishly willing to hurt the other person to gain an advantage over him, or to experience the excitement of telling about his faults.

- Conferral involves sharing information only with responsible people who may be able to help. When we confer, we solicit the advice of other Christians who share our desire to help so that we may be more effective in giving this help. Gossip involves sharing such information with whomever we please, without regard for how this might affect the ones about whom we talk.

- Conferral involves talking only about present problems, and whatever past context is necessary to accurately understand the present problem. Gossip involves talking about past problems or purely personal issues. It also neglects or even distorts the context, because it is more concerned with spreading dirt.

- Conferral includes a commitment to talk to the person about whom we are conferring if this is appropriate. Gossip delights in talking about someone rather than talking to him.

- Conferral promotes trust and openness between Christians, and correspondingly tends to reduce gossip because we model this kind of redemptive speech about each other. Gossip promotes fear and mistrust between Christians. It also promotes more gossip—Christians will still talk about each other's problems, but without an example of healthy conferral, people will tend to gossip.

When to Confer and When to Remain Silent

There are no simplistic rules for when we should confer and when we should remain silent. But there are biblical principles that, along with the personal leading of the Holy Spirit, help us to make wise decisions in this area.

Accept the Burden of Responsible Trust, but Not Confidentiality

Except where bound by legal restrictions, we should not assume that such information is confidential in the strict sense of the word. Instead, we should handle this kind of information with responsible trust. We should view another's confession as precious information, not to be shared lightly or irresponsibly. But neither should we view such information as automatically binding us to a vow of silence, because there may be good reasons to share it with others.

If another Christian shares his sin problems with me, he is trusting me to do with this information as I think is best for his welfare, as well as for the welfare of the church. The question, then, is not "Is this information confidential?" but rather "What is the most responsible and helpful way to respond?" This is really a watershed difference, because there is an assumption of openness to the resources of other Christians instead of an assumption that they are off limits.

This is one reason why, when someone says, "I want to share something with you but you must promise me first that you won't tell anyone else," I interrupt that person. I say, "I'm sorry, but I won't make that promise. I may need to tell others about what you share with me. It may be morally wrong for me to keep this information a secret. I can promise you that I will be responsible with what you tell me. But if you tell me, you must be willing to trust me to do what I think is best with this information." This response causes the other person to think through the reasons for confiding in me, and it saves me potential problems. Often, there is no need to tell others, but it is still a good opportunity for the person to learn how Christian fellowship works.

Responsible trust also means that if I deem it necessary to confer with others about this situation, I will normally tell the one who confided in me that I think this is necessary. I am not asking the person's permission to confer; I am rather letting him know that this is the best way I can help him. Of course, he is welcome to come with me to confer with another worker. I have no reason to be embarrassed or ashamed about my decision to confer because I am doing so in his best interest.

Some may think this is an outlandish way to deal with confided sins, but I have found it to be extremely helpful for everyone involved. I am free to get the help I need so I can help my brother. He is getting the added help he needs, and he is also often learning how Christians should help each other in this area. Those who really want freedom from their sins are usually willing to do whatever it takes to get this freedom. However, those who want to dictate how you must handle the information are usually confiding in you for the wrong reasons. They may want to soothe their consciences without facing their responsibility.

When deciding whether or not to confer, there are some basic guidelines that help us make this decision.

Is Someone Being Injured by Your Silence About This Situation?

Many issues are of such a purely personal nature that there is no good reason to confer with others. Many issues concern past sins that have little or no present ramifications. When this is the case, it is usually unnecessary to confer with others. Show the person God's grace and encourage him to share it with others if he feels the need because such sharing can enhance friendships.

Many sins, though, are directly affecting other individuals or the witness of the church. Consider the sin of adultery with another member of the church. The adulterer's spouse has a moral right to know about this breach of the marital vows. True marital restoration will require confession, repentance, and forgiveness. In addition, this affair may scandalize the church. To keep silent about this is to enter into a conspiracy of evil.

The correct thing to do in this situation is to insist that the confider confess this sin to his spouse, and to involve other workers in the church who can help you restore the people involved. You should offer to help him take these steps, but you should insist that he take them and make it clear that you will take this information to those who should know it if he refuses to do so. This may sound harsh, but it is the medicine that is necessary to heal a grievous wound.

What Role Does the Confider Play in the Church?

Those who play leadership roles have greater accountability to the church. If a new Christian confides to you that he abused drugs or alcohol, the issue probably doesn't need to go any further unless he wants to share it with others. But what if an elder of your church confides a similar sin to you? Because he is in a leadership position, he bears a greater responsibility to the church as a whole for this breach of trust. He is especially accountable to the other elders of the church, to confess his moral failure and submit to their plan of discipline and restoration. You should offer to help him do this, but make it clear that you will assure that it happens for the sake of the church's integrity.

In between these two scenarios are many different roles in the church: new youth worker, home group leader, public teacher. The principle to observe is that the worker is accountable to the leader(s) of the ministry in which he is working, and should therefore divulge this information to them and submit to their judgment on how to resolve it.

Why and with Whom Do You Want to Confer?

You should be able to clearly articulate to yourself why you want to confer with another person about a confided problem. Are you confused about how to help the person? Does someone else have a responsibility to know this information? Or do you just have an itch to tell someone about this juicy news? You should also be able to identify the person(s) with whom you should confer. Who has the most experience with this kind of situation? Who knows this person best? Answering these questions sometimes requires prayerful reflection, and is a good safeguard against divulging important information indiscreetly or gossiping.

How Do You Tend to Handle Such Information?

Do you tend to automatically share such information with others? If so, ask yourself why you shouldn't keep this to yourself. There may indeed be good reasons to confer with others, but you should be sure you know them before you do so. Do you tend to keep such matters to yourself when you should seek help from others? If so, you should be able to justify why you aren't conferring with another wise Christian on this matter. Are you unsure about your tendencies in this area? Why not ask another Christian worker who knows you well to give you his frank opinion about this part of your character? Such self-knowledge is vital to those who want to serve the Lord effectively.

Conclusion: Two Attitudes to Resist

Resist Gossip

As Christians, we should vigorously resist gossip in the body of Christ. All of us have gossiped, and all of us have the capacity to gossip again. Our fallen natures will always desire to use information about others to exalt ourselves at their expense. We should learn to identify this urge and judge it before we gossip.

Cultivate the habit of asking yourself, "Why do I want to talk to others about this person's sins?" It will save you much damage to others and to yourself. When we are guilty of gossiping, we should take the initiative to apologize for this and make amends as much as possible.

Without being self-righteous, we should also give short shrift to gossip about others. If you discern someone is gossiping, consider asking "Why are you telling us this?" or "What did the person say about this problem when you confronted him about it?" Perhaps you need to press him to talk with the other person instead of talking to you. Perhaps you need to urge him to drop it because it is unconstructive gossip. We should strongly discipline unrepentant gossips—potentially even to the point of barring them from our churches until they repent (Titus 3:10).

It is possible, however, to become overly scrupulous about resisting gossip. If we are involved deeply in trying to serve others, we will experience frustration with people and their problems. If you never experience this kind of frustration, you may be very mature—but probably you aren't involved deeply enough with sinful people.

Christian workers should have a way to vent these frustrations with their close friends and co-workers. Sometimes, we don't need to confer and we don't want to gossip—we just want to blow off some steam about how difficult it is to deal with someone. It simply wouldn't be normal, for example, for a wife to not express such frustrations with someone to her husband. While we can abuse this, it is one of the provisions of close friendships. But with this provision comes the responsibility to gently help each other, when necessary, into a more constructive attitude toward the frustrating person.

Resist the Right to Privacy

We should just as vigorously resist the right-to-privacy mentality. Yes, there are good reasons to urge others to be discreet about their knowledge of your sins. Yes, it is wise to not to share your problems with a proven gossip. Yes, there is sometimes a valid reason for rebuking someone who gossiped about you. But it is not possible to protect ourselves from these risks unless we are willing to sacrifice relational closeness with others.

Tragically, this is the price many people are willing to pay for their right to privacy. In the world, where non-Christians have no real basis for trusting each other, this is understandable and even expected. But it shouldn't be this way among Christians! In the body of Christ, we should value the richness of love relationships enough to risk the chance of gossip.

What is the most common reason why we don't want others to know about our sins? Isn't it our prideful desire to keep up a good front, or the desire to deal with our insecurities by controlling how others treat us? Christ has come to liberate us from this bondage. He has made us God's children and given us a new identity. Because we know God accepts us in spite of all our sinfulness, we can begin to be less self-protective and more open with others. Indeed, we need to step out in faith to do this if we want to experience more deeply the security of God's acceptance.

The Christian who says, "I am being open with God about my sins, but I won't be open with other Christians" is probably fooling himself. Openness with God will lead to openness with other Christians because, as I have argued throughout this book, God ministers to us through his body. If we are walking in the light with God, we will have open fellowship with one another (1 John 1:7).

The more spiritually mature we become individually and corporately, the more open we will become with one another about our sins. One of the signs of a healthy church is that the people know about each other's sins and problems—and still love each other. We should prefer the risk of gossip and correct it when it occurs rather than forfeit this kind of openness in our friendships with other Christians.

APPENDIX 2

Ten Keys to Successful Home Groups

The need for effective small-group ministry is implied in the New Testament. If the local church is to truly develop the spiritual gifts of its members, and mobilize the terrific power of the Holy Spirit to work through a trained and experienced laity, it will need smaller groups where training and experience can occur.

Xenos Christian Fellowship is an independent church in Columbus, Ohio, which has made much use of lay-led, small home group ministry. In fact, the home groups are the central focus of this church. The type of small-group ministry used in this case has also resulted in good morale on the part of the several hundred lay home fellowship leaders, and the hundreds of other graduates of the eighteen-month training course offered to members. Because of this success, the ministerial staff of Xenos is frequently called upon by other pastors to consult regarding the establishment and/or management of small-group lay ministry in their own churches.

Through these consultations, we discovered that small-group ministries are not a novel idea. In fact, most evangelical churches seem to have tried to establish a network of small groups at one time or another. At the same time, most of these efforts are unsuccessful to some degree. Often the question asked is "What have we been doing wrong?" Frequently the church has either canceled the home fellowship project altogether, or there are substantial problems.

The problems encountered when trying to establish a home-group ministry sometimes include a lack of participation and interest on the part of the church members. Sometimes a small minority of the church struggles along, unwilling to admit failure in the program, and developing a "faithful remnant" theology which justifies, on theological grounds, the lack of growth and lack of participation by the other members.

Frequent failures are not the result of divine opposition to the idea of small groups, or the fact that "our kind of people aren't right for this sort of thing." Instead, there are a number of good theological and practical reasons why these groups usually fail.

1. Base Home Groups on New Testament Ecclesiological Theory

Both New Testament example and principle argue for small home-sized groups as a key feature of the local church. In the area of biblical example, Acts 2:46 states that the Jerusalem church met "in the temple" and "from house to house." Concerning the meetings in the Temple, we know that Solomon's portico was probably quite large, and could have accommodated even the several thousands that were a part of the Jerusalem church.

Yet, the apostles did not consider these large meetings to be sufficient by themselves. It should be obvious that an impersonal atmosphere will result if only very large meetings are held. The network of close relationships that should characterize the community of the church requires encouragement from the local church itself through the provision of smaller group meeting formats such as those described in this passage.

In another case, Paul reminded the Ephesian elders that he had exhorted them both "publicly and from house to house" (Acts 20:20). In this passage, "publicly" probably refers to the school room of Tyrannus (Acts 19:9). It is important to see that Paul did not limit his speaking ministry to the large meeting place, even though one was available.

Paul apparently refers to several home churches in the city of Rome (Romans 16:4, 10, 11, 14, 15). In 1 Corinthians 14:35 Paul mentions "churches" in the plural, after having already referred to "the church of God which is at Corinth" (1 Corinthians 1:2) in the singular.

It seems clear from these and other references that it was common practice to have a cluster of home churches in each city, all of which continued to work together with the same elders. It is probably significant that no church buildings have been found from the earliest period of the church (A.D. 33-150), and even those from the second century were homes with a large room added on.

New Testament principles surrounding the issues of body life, spiritual gifts, and the fact that real spiritual ministry is the business of every member in the local church cannot be effectively brought into practice in a large group setting (see Romans 12; 1 Corinthians 12, 14; Ephesians 4:11-16; Colossians 2:19). It is necessary to provide smaller group settings where relationships can grow between members. Then the members will be able to discover each other's needs, and will be able to meet those needs on an individual level.

Unfortunately, when churches attempt to initiate a small-group ministry, they sometimes fail to teach the people that the purpose of the meeting is to practice these biblical principles. The result is sometimes a wrong impression on the part of most participants. Members often feel that the meeting is primarily intended as a social gathering, or a place where "my needs can be met," rather than "a place where I can develop a ministry."

The first order of business in beginning this kind of ministry is to launch a teaching offensive in the church. The goal would be to establish an understanding and a vision of New Testament ecclesiology in the minds of the participants.

2. Follow Correct Criteria When Selecting Leaders

The Bible teaches that spiritual criteria must be used to select leaders. The qualifications of a deacon (1 Timothy 3:8-13) would serve well for the initial selection of leaders of home fellowship group. Too often, however, the church will designate men and women for leadership on the basis of secular abilities, job status, levels of financial giving, or seniority in the church. The result is usually a meeting that is not very spiritually edifying or appealing.

After leaders have been selected on the basis of character and knowledge, they should also be evaluated on the basis of actual function, or role. When Jesus says "my sheep hear my voice," he is giving us a basic way to recognize a good shepherd. A Christian's leadership cannot be considered authentic until someone is willing to follow him or her.

In many churches, it may be very difficult to determine who our authentic leaders are. This is because there has not been ample opportunity for them to try their hand at leadership. In these cases, we will have to pick leaders on the basis of the best criteria possible. Later, when lay-led groups are in place, it should be possible to evaluate the effectiveness of the work done by the more committed members of the group. Other things being equal, the more effective workers should be the first to be moved forward.

3. Give Real Authority to the Leaders

If the home fellowship is to be fashioned after the biblical examples of house churches, then the leaders of the groups should be allowed to run their groups the way the leaders of the New Testament house churches ran theirs. In the New Testament, the authors admonish their readers to respect their leaders and to follow their lead in the running of the home church (1 Cor. 16:16; Heb. 13:17; 1 Thess. 5:14).

Sometimes, churches impose a structure upon the small group that is too restrictive. This structure may include a preplanned curriculum for study, and a long list of policy restrictions. The effect is usually to stifle initiative and sap motivation. The leaders realize very quickly that they are functioning as agents for the existing leadership of the church, but that they themselves are leaders in name only. When the church requires the home-group leaders to check in on virtually all decisions, it clearly suggests that they are incompetent to make their own decisions. (Sometimes they are incompetent, but the church must bear responsibility for this as well).

It is usually not desirable to forsake all control over the actions of home fellowship leaders, because lay leaders are usually not as well trained as professional pastors. Therefore, it is necessary to carefully weigh which areas are left to the discretion of the home leaders, and which areas need to be cleared with the higher authority of the church. The point in making this decision is to arrive at a balance that will prevent serious errors from occurring (even though there is never a guarantee that all problems can be prevented), while delegating real decision-making authority to the home fellowship leaders.

4. Cultivate an Outreach Focus

Small groups are often established with the ultimate goal of fellowship rather than evangelism. While quality fellowship is one of the rewards of small-group ministry, it is an inadequate basis for any Christian group. If we have only fellowship as our goal, the group is essentially self-centered, or self-focused. Thus, it is no surprise that such groups are prone to division and discontent. This is because outreach and mission are the natural context within which fellowship should occur. When a group of people occupy themselves with each other to the exclusion of the outside world, discontent is sure to follow. We should be unwilling to consider the option of handling all outreach at the large meeting and limiting small groups to an exclusively fellowship role. If home groups are for Christians only, then they must see their goal as incorporating new Christians, and there should be some mechanism for finding and inviting these new Christians from the large meeting.

The fact that Acts 2:46 says that the Jerusalem church was "breaking bread from house to house" but does not mention evangelism is a moot point, since the passage does not mention where evangelism did occur. On the other hand, in 1 Corinthians 14:24, Paul clearly contemplates "unbelievers" entering an interactive meeting—apparently a home church (see v. 26, 34).

5. Make Provision for Church Discipline

In cases where home fellowships are established with no provision for church discipline, a very distressing and familiar pattern emerges. Some people are attracted to small groups for the wrong reasons. There are those who come to exploit others, or simply to use the group to become the center of attention.

The impact of such people is greater in a small group than it would be in a large meeting. As a result, the whole character of the group can be altered to such an extent that it becomes difficult to attract new people, or even to hold the interest and loyalty of the productive members.

The New Testament provides a solution to this kind of situation. Those members who are willing to damage others or themselves are to be confronted in love about their attitude and/or actions (see 1 Thessalonians 5:14; Matthew 18:15). If they are not responsive, a legitimate amount of pressure can be applied—even to the point of removing them from the group.

According to the Bible, this kind of discipline in love is not optional, although, of course, the application of it should be gracious, and suited to the needs of the individual, as well as the group. In order to prevent abuses or legalism, the eldership should be consulted in cases where an ultimatum may be issued.

6. Leaders and Workers Should Be Accountable for Their Ministry

The Bible indicates that along with the privilege of being in authority comes the responsibility of being under authority. This is one of the reasons for the New Testament practice of having group leadership in the local church (see Acts 14:23; Titus 1:5; 1 Peter 5:2, "among you"). Although no one would try to run a business without accountability, this principle is often not instituted when home fellowships are set up, because a single leader is put in charge of each home group.

The model that holds the home group leader accountable to the higher leadership of the church is inadequate. There is also need to have those on the spot who can dissent or agree. When pastors or elders try to run small groups from a distance, they have no real way of knowing what is going on. Neither is there time to regularly visit each group to find out how things are going.

Thus we find that home fellowship groups that are set up without group leadership run into destructive problems. The leaders become relatively easy targets of satanic attack. The balance that usually results from group interaction in a leaders meeting is missing–sometimes resulting in doctrinal extremes, or other abuses. In addition, leaders and/or workers who are not regularly reporting to each other on their work, may stop doing their work, or may miss important opportunities.

A unified core of leaders is a good safeguard against overreaction and division. The leaders should be admonished to learn to get along with each other. In cases where they are unable to agree, they should seek arbitration from an elder or other recognized church leader.

7. Offer Adequate Equipping for Would-be Leaders

The Bible does not allow the local church the option of telling its people to go away for their training. According to Ephesians 4:11,12, it is the responsibility of the leadership of the local church to provide quality training in Christian work ("the work of service") to its own people. When the leadership of a church decides not to have a small group ministry because its "laymen" are too ignorant, this is not an excuse—it is an admission of guilt.

For many churches, the first step toward a successful home fellowship ministry would be the establishment of a full year-long course of in-depth theological and practical ministry training for the proposed leaders.

If there is already an adequate supply of leaders who have some biblical knowledge, it would be preferable to hold this training while home groups are in progress, so they can immediately use the knowledge they learn. This prevents the accumulation of dead knowledge and also avoids creating the impression that Christian work is more difficult than it really is.

At the same time, it should be made clear that completion of the training course will not necessarily result in an assignment as a home group leader. That decision will have to also depend on other considerations such as character development, and a record of self-sacrificing service to others.

8. Set Multiplication Goals and Devise a Plan for Multiplying Home Groups

In many cases, a home fellowship's existence is viewed as an end in itself. As mentioned earlier, this lack of mission-mindedness has a negative effect on the group. On the other hand, good small groups tend not to stay small. Thus, when a house fills up with people, the group tends to lose much of its interactive character. In addition, outreach tends to dwindle because there is no room for new people. In cases like this, it is natural to divide the group in order to preserve the small size of the group, while at the same time, reaching more people.

Unless a plan is devised for multiplication that encourages outreach, discipleship, and equipping, home fellowships tend to resist multiplication. Church leaders should establish ground rules established which help to insure success for both new groups, with a minimum of disruption to the relationships that have been developed. Otherwise, the system will tend to stifle initiative and punish success. In other words, the view of the leaders might well be, "the faster our group grows, the sooner we get to part ways with the close friends we have made so far."

9. View Home Groups as Central to the Life of the Church

In some churches, the large worship meeting and/or teaching meetings are viewed as essential, but the home group is considered an option—helpful to some, but not necessarily normative for healthy involvement in the local church.

As pointed out earlier, this view ignores the biblical point of view that the local body depends on the individual function of each and every member (Ephesians 4:15,16). We should resist the temptation to dilute this teaching (for instance, teaching that giving money on Sunday, or serving as an usher is the intent of this passage). If we allow this understanding of the church to predominate, there will be no strong motivation to exercise real spiritual gifts, or to help small group ministry succeed.

If the church fails to establish a vision for full involvement in the minds of its members, it will result in a very poor level of participation in the home fellowship program. Often, only those with little to do will spend the time it takes to become meaningfully involved. To obtain the help of our most gifted members, we will need to teach that involvement in home group mission and fellowship is an exciting opportunity to finally realize the full extent of normal Christian experience.

It is the responsibility of the leadership in the local church to cultivate a consensus in the church which places an appropriate emphasis on this kind of ministry. Such a consensus can be created without resorting to legalism. It is only necessary that the leadership truly believe in the concept themselves, and are willing to teach and practice it in their own lives.

10. Pastors Should View Home Groups as an Opportunity Rather Than as a Threat

There can be several reasons why pastors are threatened by lay-led home groups. There are dangers in the area of false teaching. However, this is why the Bible teaches the need for "overseers" or elders. The elders should also train the "lay" work force so that they will be able to teach sound doctrine.

It is possible that some leaders prefer the control they have when they are the only leaders in the church. This feeling is understandable, especially when a pastor is already having trouble controlling the church. However, a home-group ministry of this type would not increase the work load of the pastor in the long run. The key to maintaining quality ministry, even for a growing church, is to delegate work to other members.

The man or woman of God must pass judgment on his or her own attitude, admitting that a willingness to inhibit others' ministry for the sake of establishing his or her own is most censurable. The fact that we may feel threatened in our position in the church is no excuse. We have been placed where we are in order to facilitate others' ministry, not to inhibit it.

There is no basis for such a fear. The lesson learned at Xenos during the past several years is that the New Testament model is not only theologically correct—it is also capable of yielding New Testament results. During that time, Xenos has multiplied dozens of home groups. After beginning in 1976 with only 60 people, there are today over 5000 students and adults regularly attending home groups. Furthermore, the home groups have spread out to different areas of the city, reaching different kinds of people in their own neighborhoods.

Endnotes

Chapter 1

1. For example, in Mark 5:15 after the man from the Gerasenes had been delivered from demonic possession, he is described as being "in his right mind." This term sophronounta is the same word used by Paul in Romans 12:3.

2. John White, The Fight (Downers Grove: InterVarsity Press, 1979), pp. 149-150.

3. Francis A. Schaeffer, The Church at the End of the 20th Century (Downers Grove: InterVarsity Press, 1972), pp. 139-140.

Chapter 2

1. Perhaps Paul learned his identity as a member of Christ's body even during his conversion. When he was struck down by Jesus on his way to Damascus to arrest Christians he cried out, "Who are you, Lord?" Jesus' answer, "I am Jesus, whom you are persecuting," communicated his essential union with all true Christians. Although Jesus struck Paul blind through a direct encounter, he healed Paul and commissioned him as an apostle through Ananias. Through these words and actions Jesus revealed the essential truth of his body to Paul from the outset of his dealings with him.

Chapter 3

1. D. A. Carson, The Gospel According to John (Grand Rapids: Zondervan Publishing House, 1991), p. 462.

2. Paul quotes Jesus in a similar statement in Acts 20:35: "It is more blessed (makarios) to give than to receive."

Chapter 4

1. Paraklesis (the noun) is used twenty-three times in the New Testament epistles. Parakaleo (the verb) is used fifty-four times.

2. See, for example, Xenophon Anab. 3.1.32: "they called in the general." Cited in Colin Brown, ed., Dictionary of New Testament Theology, vol. 1 (Grand Rapids: Zondervan Publishing House 1981) p. 569.

Chapter 5

1. See Appendix 1 for an extensive treatment of this issue.

Chapter 6

1. Catechism of the Catholic Church (Ligouri, Mo.: Libreria Editrice Vaticana, 1994), p. 373.

2. The exact meaning of this verse is difficult to determine. The previous context seems to involve physical sickness, which can sometimes be a discipline from God to urge us to repent (see 1 Corinthians 11:30-32). In this case, verse 16 would describe how we should respond to such discipline so that we may be physically healed. But it is also possible that in verse 16 James is drawing a more general conclusion from his specific instructions in verses 14 and 15. He may be teaching us that mutual confession and prayer is one of the means God has provided for our moral and spiritual healing.

3. See Howard Snyder, The Radical Wesley (Downers Grove: InterVarsity Press, 1980), pp. 59-60. See also A. Skevington Wood, The Burning Heart (Minneapolis: Bethany Fellowship, 1978), p. 192.

4. See Appendix 1 on confidentiality.

Chapter 7

1. Sometimes the occasion of bitterness is an imagined offense—something that the bitter person perceives as an offense, but that did not happen, or that God's Word does not condemn. For example, some children become embittered at one of their parents because their other parent lied about their character. Some children are bitter toward their parents because they were disciplined for just cause, but refuse to acknowledge their poor behavior. In the case of bitterness over imagined offenses, the resolution is not forgiveness but acknowledging that there was no offense.

2. Solomon warns us not to so this. "Like one who takes a dog by the ears is he who passes by and meddles with strife not belonging to him" (Proverbs 26:17). "Do not contend with a man without cause, if he has done you no harm" (Proverbs 3:30).

3. "Do not gloat when your enemy falls; when he stumbles, do not let your heart rejoice" (Proverbs 24:17).

4. This is not to suggest that bitterness is the only cause of depression. There are many other causes, including chemical imbalance. Those who experience chronic or severe depression should seek professional help to discover the cause(s) of their depression.

5. David W. Augsburger, The Freedom of Forgiveness (Chicago: Moody Press, 1988).

Chapter 8

1. "The point is that for the central core of the Christian faith—what C. S. Lewis called 'mere' Christianity—the biblical evidence is overwhelming. The deity of Christ, the triune nature of God, the creation of the world by God, the sinfulness of all humanity, salvation by grace through faith, the resurrection of the dead—these and many other such matters are clearly taught in scripture." James Sire, Scripture Twisting (Downers Grove: InterVarsity Press, 1980), pp. 12-13.

2. Francis A. Schaeffer, The Complete Works of Francis Schaeffer (Westchester, Ill.: Crossway books, 1982), vol. 4, p. 34.

3. Paul's response to the dietary and religious-day dispute among Roman Christians is instructive at this point. Paul clearly sided with those who declared their freedom to eat all foods and not observe any days as having intrinsic spiritual significance. After all, he calls those who hold this position the "strong in faith." He also defended this position because it was strategically important for reaching Gentiles for Christ (1 Cor. 9:19-23). But, in spite of this, he warns the "strong" against condemning the "weak"—because they answer ultimately to Christ and because they showed evidence of serving Christ: "He who observes the day, observes it for the Lord, ...and he who eats not, for the Lord he does not eat, and gives thanks to God. For not one of us lives for himself, and not one dies for himself; for if we live, we live for the Lord, or if we die, we die for the Lord; therefore whether we live or die, we are the Lord's. For to this end Christ died and lived again, that He might be Lord both of the dead and of the living. But you, why do you judge your brother? Or you again, why do you regard your brother with contempt? For we shall all stand before the judgment seat of God" (Rom. 14:6-10).

4. According to George Gallup, while 88 percent of American evangelicals believe that "the Bible is the written word of God, accurate in all that it teaches," 53 percent of the same respondents believe "there is no such thing as absolute truth." See Gene Edward Veith, Postmodern Times (Wheaton, Ill.: Crossway Books, 1994), p. 16.

5. This was clearly Paul's intent in Colossians 2:16–23, where he warns his audience not to let certain teachers impose ritual, dietary, or ascetic stipulations on their view of Christian spirituality.

6. Even though Paul says in 1 Corinthians 8:13, "if food causes my brother to stumble, I will never eat meat again," the following context makes it clear that he is calling for them to not eat meat in the presence of the weaker ones. "Eat anything that is sold in the meat market, without asking questions for conscience' sake; for the earth is the Lord's, and all it contains. If one of the unbelievers invites you, and you wish to go, eat anything that is set before you, without asking questions for conscience' sake. But if anyone should say to you, 'This is meat sacrificed to idols,' do not eat it, for the sake of the one who informed you, and for conscience' sake; I mean not your own conscience, but the other man's; for why is my freedom judged by another's

conscience? If I partake with thankfulness, why am I slandered concerning that for which I give thanks?" (1 Cor. 10:23-30).

Chapter 9

1. My own church does not have a formal membership for this reason. Since the Bible teaches that all true Christians are automatically members of the church, we feel it is somewhat confusing to have a membership for our own local expression of Christ's body. Why not keep the emphasis on receiving Christ and healthy involvement in the local church?

2, See Appendix 2 for a fuller treatment of these keys.

3 See for example, Robert Coleman, The Master Plan of Evangelism (Old Tappan, N.J.: Fleming H. Revell, 1987); Leroy Eims, The Lost Art of Disciple-Making (Grand Rapids: Zondervan Publishing House, 1982); Leroy Eims, Laboring in the Harvest (Colorado Springs: Navpress, 1985); Waylon Moore, Multiplying Disciples (Colorado Springs: Navpress, 1981); Christopher Adsit, Personal Disciple-Making (San Bernardino: Here's Life Publishers, Inc., 1988); Dennis McCallum and Jessica Lowery, Organic Discipleship (New Paradigm Publishing, 2006).

4 See Kenneth C. Kinghorn, Discovering Your Spiritual Gifts (Grand Rapids, Francis Asbury Press, 1981); Bruce L. Bugbee, Networking (Pasadena: Charles E. Fuller Institute, 1991); Robert E. Logan and Janet Logan, Spiritual Gifts Implementation: Moving from. Gifts Discovery to Ministry Placement (Pasadena: Fuller Evangelistic Association, 1986).

5. Howard Snyder, The Problem of Wineskins (Downers Grove: InterVarsity Press, 1975), pp. 106-107.

6 I have emphasized the local church in this chapter not because involvement with Christians outside this setting is wrong or unimportant but because life-changing involvement in Christian fellowship and ministry grows from this kind of healthy involvement in one's local church.

Appendix 1

1. This appendix discusses confidentiality as it relates to informal, personal relationships between Christians. There are, of course, certain settings in which we are legally obligated to divulge information or respect confidentiality. Many state laws require paid church staff to report child abuse. Professional counselors are usually required to observe strict confidentiality concerning most information divulged by their clients. Readers are advised to learn and observe their legal responsibilities in their specific and professional roles.

You can receive more information about Christian relationships, home groups, Xenos Christian Fellowship, and many other quality Christian ministry materials by visiting our web site: http://www.xenos.org